AN ASSET BUILDER'S GUIDE TO
SERVICE-LEARNING

T 83408

Search
INSTITUTE

Practical research benefiting children and youth

D1122216

An Asset Builder's Guide to Service-Learning was developed with the generous support of
The Lilly Endowment as part of Habits of the Heart: Strengthening Traditions of Giving and
Serving, an initiative of the Indiana Humanities Council. A pilot version of this resource was
developed as part of Uniting Congregations for Youth Development, a four-year initiative
funded by the DeWitt Wallace-Reader's Digest Fund.

Additional support comes from Search Institute's Healthy Communities • Healthy Youth initiative.
This initiative seeks to motivate and equip individuals, organizations, and their leaders to join
together in nurturing competent, caring, and responsible children and adolescents. This mission
will be accomplished through research, evaluation, resource materials, training, technical assistance,
and networking opportunities based on Search Institute's framework of developmental assets.

Major corporate support for Search Institute's Healthy Communities • Healthy Youth initiative
is provided by Lutheran Brotherhood, a member-owned organization of more than one million
Lutherans joined together for financial security, benevolent outreach, and volunteer service.
Lutheran Brotherhood demonstrates its stewardship through programs that serve Lutherans,
strengthen communities, and aid Lutheran congregations and institutions.

AN ASSET BUILDER'S GUIDE TO SERVICE-LEARNING

Search Institute
700 South Third Street, Suite 210
Minneapolis, MN 55415
612-376-8955
800-888-7828
www.search-institute.org

10   9   8   7   6   5   4   3   2   1

ISBN: 1-57482-114-8

CREDITS
Contributors: Eugene C. Roehlkepartain, Thomas Bright, and Beth Margolis-Rupp
Editors: Jennifer Griffin-Wiesner, Mary Byers, and Lynn Ingrid Nelson
Text design: Diane Gleba Hall
Cover design: Nancy Wester
Production Coordinator: Jeannie Dressel

CONTENTS

CONTENTS

FIGURES, TABLES, AND WORKSHEETS

INTRODUCTION

EXPLORING CONNECTIONS

In recent years, more and more young people have been leaving their classrooms, places of worship, and youth centers to make a difference in the "real world." They are finding out how what they study and the beliefs they hold connect with social issues of the day. They are learning about challenges facing their communities and how they can be part of the solutions. They are realizing that they can be depended on to do important work. They are exploring personal interests and career possibilities. In short, young people are discovering the power and benefit of serving others for shaping who they are and who they are becoming.

Recent decades have seen a dramatic expansion in the field of youth service. Schools across the country have adopted service-learning as a core educational strategy that links hands-on experience addressing real-world issues with the school's curriculum. Community agencies have begun innovative approaches for integrating children and youth into their volunteer activities. Youth organizations have integrated service-learning as a core component of their youth development programming. Congregations and denominations have seen a dramatic increase in youth involvement in summer work trips and other service activities. (See Figure 1 for research on young people's involvement in service-related activities.)

This widespread interest in engaging young people in service to others represents a tremendous opportunity for "asset builders"—people who are committed to ensuring that all young people have in their lives the basic building blocks they need for healthy development. Not only is service to others one of the 40 developmental assets that Search Institute has identified as a critical building block for child and adolescent development, but service-learning, if done well, can nurture many of the developmental assets.

This guide assists youth workers, educators, and community builders in making the connections between asset building and service-learning. Two beliefs undergird this resource:

1. Service-learning can be a core strategy for building developmental assets in multiple settings within a community; and

2. The framework of developmental assets can be used to strengthen service-learning efforts.

Thus, this guide is intended to assist those who seek to develop strategies for doing service-learning in ways that maximize its asset-building potential. This requires integrating insights and effective practices of service-learning with the basic principles of asset building. These tools are designed both to strengthen existing service-learning efforts and to assist people dedicated to asset building in effectively utilizing service-learning in their efforts.

FIGURE 1

FACTS AND FIGURES ON SERVING OTHERS

Independent Sector estimates that 13.3 million teenagers volunteered formally or informally in 1995, giving 1.8 billion hours—an estimated value of $7.7 billion.[1]

HOW MUCH TIME DO HIGH SCHOOL SENIORS SPEND SERVING OTHERS?

More than 70 percent of high school seniors say they participate in community affairs or volunteer work, but most do it infrequently.*

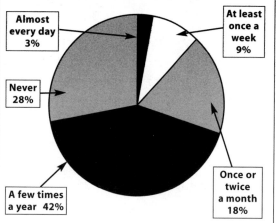

Almost every day 3%

At least once a week 9%

Never 28%

A few times a year 42%

Once or twice a month 18%

*Based on a 1995 *Monitoring the Future* survey of 2,650 high school seniors.[2]

THE GENDER DIFFERENCE

Adolescent girls are more likely to serve others regularly than adolescent boys, as the following chart shows.*

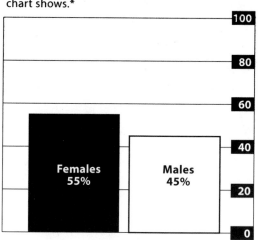

Females 55%

Males 45%

*Percentages of young people who report serving in the community one or more hours per week, according to Search Institute surveys of almost 100,000 youth in 213 communities.[3]

THE AGE DIFFERENCE

As young people move through middle and high school, they become less likely to serve others.*

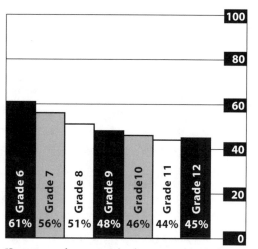

Grade 6 61% Grade 7 56% Grade 8 51% Grade 9 48% Grade 10 46% Grade 11 44% Grade 12 45%

*Percentages of young people who report serving in the community one or more hours per week, according to Search Institute surveys of almost 100,000 youth in 213 communities.[4]

YOUTH FROM ALL BACKGROUNDS SERVE OTHERS

Similar proportions of young people from all racial/ethnic backgrounds report serving others at least one hour a week.*

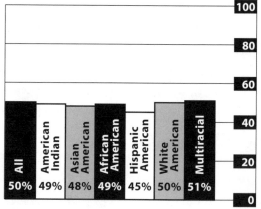

All 50% American Indian 49% Asian American 48% African American 49% Hispanic American 45% White American 50% Multiracial 51%

*Percentages of young people who report serving in the community one or more hours per week, according to Search Institute surveys of almost 100,000 youth in 213 communities.[5]

How this Guide Is Organized

This guide is divided into two major sections:

A. Laying the Foundation for Asset-Based Service-Learning—The first four chapters examine foundational issues in linking service-learning and asset building. The first chapter explains both concepts and builds bridges between them. Chapter 2 looks at issues of leadership and organizational support. Chapter 3 suggests ways of shaping service-learning efforts to include children, adolescents, families, and intergenerational groups, as well as youth with disabilities and vulnerable youth—young people who are often overlooked as resources for their organizations and communities. Finally, Chapter 4 presents essential issues in setting a stage for service-learning, such as establishing goals and ensuring safety and funding.

B. PARR: A Basic Service-Learning Process—The second part of the guide presents a basic process for effective service-learning, which we call PARR. As shown in Figure 2, this model highlights four key elements of service-learning.

This process is an important lens for service-learning, calling for an appropriate balance between the four elements. For example, leaders sometimes put most of their energy into the *act* of serving (action), thinking that the learning will follow naturally. Yet that rarely happens very effectively; intentional efforts to encourage reflection are key to the learning being internalized. These chapters offer specific suggestions, worksheets, and tools to guide you through the process.

Who This Guide Is For

Although there are exceptions, most of the available resources on service-learning are designed primarily for schools. This book is unique in that it is designed for leaders who seek to engage young people in service-learning in many different settings, including schools, youth organizations, and congregations. While there are obvious differences between these settings, each shares much in common: a commitment to young people, an emphasis on learning (whether it's formal, religious, or informal), and an interest in the wider community. Furthermore, the basic principles of effective service-learning apply to all contexts, not just schools.

Another group who will find this book helpful are people who are involved in community-wide asset-building initiatives, or Healthy Communities • Healthy Youth initiatives. Service-learning does not have to be confined to a single organization or institution. In fact, because many sectors in a community value service-learning as a strategy, it offers the potential for community-wide service experiences for youth and intergenerational groups. In his book *All Kids Are Our Kids*, Search Institute president Peter L. Benson outlines a vision of a healthy community that includes many opportunities to serve:

> *While social activities, block parties, and other opportunities [for] helping people form relationships play an important role in an asset-building community, they cannot alone cultivate the deeper bonds and commitments out of which true community emerges. A key strategy . . . is to engage residents of all ages in service to the community. These experiences can be powerful in providing assistance to others and enhancing a person's own relationships and competencies.*[6]

This book will help leaders and other initiative participants find and maximize the potential of service-learning opportunities in their community.

How to Use This Guide

We've designed this resource as a workbook and have included plenty of ideas, suggestions, and worksheets. While you can certainly choose to jump

FIGURE 2

THE PARR PROCESS FOR SERVICE-LEARNING

The PARR process for service-learning outlines the key phases in organizing a service-learning project or program. Effective programs put energy into all four areas.

Preparation involves everything from selecting a project to preparing young people with the knowledge and skills they need to be effective. Preparation gets young people ready to serve by giving them a basic understanding of what they will be doing and why. Some preparation tasks include building enthusiasm, selecting a project, introducing social issues, and preparing young people and others to serve. Preparation is the focus of Chapter 5.

Recognition is a time to celebrate and, more important, to figure out what's next. It reinforces young people's experiences and sets the stage for their ongoing involvement and commitment. Some recognition tasks include celebrating the experiences and sharing learnings and commitments with others. Recognition is the focus of Chapter 8.

Action focuses on the times when service is being performed—when the action is happening. Action moves social issues from young people's heads into their hearts and hands. Some action tasks include providing a supportive environment, coping with change, ensuring safety, building relationships with people being served, and documenting the experience. Action is the focus of Chapter 6.

Reflection is the intentional process of guiding young people to discover and interpret the meaning and learning from their experiences of serving others. Reflection is key to the "learning" side of service-learning. Some reflection tasks include remembering the experience, identifying issues that surfaced and skills used, exploring possibilities, and assessing what worked and what didn't. Reflection is the focus of Chapter 7.

around and use different pieces of the book at different times, it is important to emphasize that service-learning is a process with multiple components that contribute to its effectiveness. So while you may be able to get some practical ideas by looking just at Chapter 6 on action, your experience will not have the impact you may hope for if that action isn't done within the context of preparation, reflection, and recognition.

At the same time, you will find many places where you can "dip in" for the information you need at a particular time. Feel free to use the ideas in ways that fit your situation and your experience.

If you are new to service-learning we recommend following the steps outlined in this book and making adjustments as needed. You will likely find the second section of the book most helpful in its overview of the basic service-learning process.

If you have experience in service-learning, many themes in the guide will seem familiar to you, and it can serve as a reminder of effective practices. One unique feature is the integration of developmental assets throughout the manuscript. Chapter 1 offers perspectives on how this asset-building focus may serve to strengthen your efforts.

A Starting Point

No resource can address all questions and issues—particularly when it covers the multiple settings of schools, congregations, and youth organizations. However, we hope that you will find tools, ideas, and processes that help you start—or strengthen—your efforts to build assets through service-learning.

CHAPTER 1

BUILDING ASSETS THROUGH
SERVICE-LEARNING

In building a bridge, it is important first to establish foundations on either side of the river. Similarly, before linking service-learning and asset building, we must establish a foundational understanding of each concept. This chapter presents basic information about service-learning and about asset building. Then it explores both how service-learning contributes to asset building and how asset building contributes to service-learning.

Service-Learning: Learning While Contributing

The Alliance for Service-Learning in Education defines service-learning as "a method by which young people learn and develop through active participation in thoughtfully organized service experiences."[1] However, it does not have a universally accepted definition. As Robert Shumer of the National Service-Learning Clearinghouse concludes, "Service-learning is still very much an amorphous concept which continues to resist rigid definitions and universal understanding."[2]

For some, it is primarily a method for experiential education. Others think of it as a program type, whereas still others emphasize it as a philosophy. Furthermore, most conversations about defining the terms have focused on the education setting; much less attention has been paid to defining the concept

from the perspective of youth organizations, congregations, or communities. However, the basic components of service-learning transcend settings and sectors:

- **Service**—Young people engage in activities that meet the needs of others and the community; and
- **Learning**—The experiences of serving others are used as an opportunity for self-reflection and learning.

Service-learning has become a guiding philosophy for many elementary schools, middle schools, high schools, and colleges. Indeed, a growing number of schools require community service as a prerequisite for graduation.

More recently, congregations and youth-serving organizations have begun adapting community service activities by adding a learning component and enhancing what they teach by incorporating hands-on, practical experiences. In short, serving others connects to each institution's own focus for learning and growth. Consider these examples:

- During a unit on human growth and development, science students in Louisville, Kentucky, observe firsthand different ends of the human development spectrum as they volunteer in day-care centers and nursing homes. Issues such as language development, motor skills, and dementia take on real meaning and human faces.
- Youth from congregations in Albuquerque, New

Mexico, participate in a computer recycling project in which they refurbish donated computers from local businesses and provide them to local nonprofit and religious organizations. Working alongside computer professionals, the young people learn computer skills while also contributing to their community.

■ Each year, the youth committee at the Regional Youth/Adult Substance Abuse Project (RYASAP) in Bridgeport, Connecticut, designs its own service projects that teach young people about real-world issues. One year, the group developed an HIV/AIDS peer education program in which it sponsored a conference on the topic (with a youth keynote speaker) and organized a benefit fashion show that raised $1,800 for a local AIDS hospice.[3]

These are just a few examples of how creative teachers and leaders can enhance the educational aspect of service projects and strengthen learning through hands-on experience. And while each of these groups has a unique focus and reason for being together, they also all have something in common: they participate in classes or programs that use service-learning as a way of building knowledge, skills, and experience while also contributing to the

well-being of others. And, as Figure 3 suggests, this involvement has benefits throughout the community.

The potential benefits of service-learning are many. But researchers and practitioners have found that all service-learning experiences are not equal. For example, in analyzing the results of a Search Institute study of school-based service-learning among middle school students, researcher Peter C. Scales writes: "The students who were involved in high-quality, well-run service-learning programs fared better than their peers who were in lesser-quality programs or did no service-learning. The best service-learning experiences included plenty of service and a substantial amount of time for students to reflect through writing and discussions with peers, teachers, parents, community members, and others."[4]

This study is just one in a growing body of research that points to elements of service-learning programs and activities that make them most effective in shaping young people's lives. In addition, several groups in the field of service-learning have developed sets of principles for effective practice in service-learning. One such framework is shown in Figure 4. These principles, though not explicitly followed throughout this guide, undergird the scope and shape of this resource. They are also highly congruent with asset building.

Developmental Assets: A Foundation for Healthy Development

While service-learning is an educational strategy and type of youth programming undergirded by a strong philosophy of youth empowerment, developmental assets represent a foundational philosophy for understanding a broad spectrum of what young people need to be successful in life. As such, many different types of actions and strategies—from service-learning to mentoring to peer helping to neighborhood building to parent education and

FIGURE 3

SOME BENEFITS OF SERVICE-LEARNING

"Any child is capable of a lot—usually much more than we expect of them. Students, communities, and agencies all benefit from service-learning initiatives. There are no losing propositions here."

— Janet Shuster, service-learning coordinator, Kirkwood, Missouri

There are many good, general reasons for engaging youth in asset-based service-learning. Here are a few examples of the benefits:

For the Participating Young People

▶ Engaging in service to others can build many of the developmental assets, which provide a foundation for healthy development and choices.

▶ Service-Learning changes others' perceptions of young people from problems to resources.

▶ It helps them learn through active, hands-on experiences and develops their leadership potential.

▶ It connects them with caring and responsible adults and peers.

For the Sponsoring Organization

▶ Service-learning provides a potentially powerful strategy for fulfilling their mission, whether it's learning (schools), personal development (youth organizations), or growth in faith (congregations).

▶ It keeps young people engaged, connected, motivated, and excited about participation in learning and other activities.

▶ It provides a service to the community and those in need.

▶ It can energize the whole organization as young people's passion, commitment, and enthusiasm rub off on other people.

For the Recipients of Service

▶ Service-learning meets real needs.

▶ It provides an opportunity for them to build relationships with young people.

▶ It can offer new hope, encouragement, and confidence in the goodwill of others.

For the Larger Community

▶ Young people bring new energy, capabilities, and creative ideas for building community and addressing specific needs.

▶ Service-learning cultivates a new generation of caring and experienced activists and volunteers.

▶ Young people are seen as valuable resources for the community.

FIGURE 4

PRINCIPLES OF GOOD PRACTICE
FOR COMBINING SERVICE AND LEARNING

A widely recognized set of principles for effective service-learning was developed at a Wingspread conference in October 1989. This group identified 10 principles that "are a statement of what we believe are essential components of good practice."

These principles "reflect the grassroots experience and the thinking of thousands of people, hundreds of programs and numerous national organizations over the last several decades. They are offered with the hope that current initiatives to create service programs will benefit from a rich recent history." An effective service-learning program:

1. Engages people in responsible and challenging actions for the common good;

2. Provides structured opportunities for people to reflect critically on their service experience;

3. Articulates clear service and learning goals for everyone involved;

4. Allows for those with needs to define those needs;

5. Clarifies the responsibilities of each person and organization involved;

6. Matches service providers and service needs through a process that recognizes changing circumstances;

7. Expects genuine, active, and sustained organizational commitment;

8. Includes training, supervision, monitoring, support, recognition, and evaluation to meet service and learning goals;

9. Ensures that the time commitment for service and learning is flexible, appropriate, and in the best interests of all involved; and

10. Is committed to program participation by and with diverse populations.

Adapted with permission from Ellen Porter Honnet and Susan J. Poulsen, *Principles of Good Practice for Combining Service and Learning: A Wingspread Special Report* (Racine, WI: The Johnson Foundation, 1989). Also see *Standards of Quality for School-Based and Community-Based Service-Learning* (Washington, DC: Alliance for Service-Learning in Education Reform, 1995).

FIGURE 5

SEARCH INSTITUTE'S 40 DEVELOPMENTAL ASSETS

Search Institute has identified the following building blocks of healthy development that help young people grow up healthy, caring, and responsible.

EXTERNAL ASSETS

Support

1. Family support—Family life provides high levels of love and support.

2. Positive family communication—Young person and her or his parent(s) communicate positively, and young person is willing to seek advice and counsel from parent(s).

3. Other adult relationships—Young person receives support from three or more nonparent adults.

4. Caring neighborhood—Young person experiences caring neighbors.

5. Caring school climate—School provides a caring, encouraging environment.

6. Parent involvement in schooling—Parent(s) are actively involved in helping young person succeed in school.

Empowerment

7. Community values youth—Young person perceives that adults in the community value youth.

8. Youth as resources—Young people are given useful roles in the community.

9. Service to others—Young person serves in the community one hour or more per week.

10. Safety—Young person feels safe at home, school, and in the neighborhood.

Boundaries and Expectations

11. Family boundaries—Family has clear rules and consequences and monitors the young person's whereabouts.

12. School boundaries—School provides clear rules and consequences.

13. Neighborhood boundaries—Neighbors take responsibility for monitoring young people's behavior.

14. Adult role models—Parent(s) and other adults model positive, responsible behavior.

15. Positive peer influence—Young person's best friends model responsible behavior.

16. High expectations—Both parent(s) and teachers encourage the young person to do well.

Constructive Use of Time

17. Creative activities—Young person spends three or more hours per week in lessons or practice in music, theater, or other arts.

18. Youth programs—Young person spends three or more hours per week in sports, clubs, or organizations at school and/or in the community.

19. Religious community—Young person spends one or more hours per week in activities in a religious institution.

20. Time at home—Young person is out with friends "with nothing special to do" two or fewer nights per week.

INTERNAL ASSETS

Commitment to Learning

21. Achievement motivation—Young person is motivated to do well in school.

22. School engagement—Young person is actively engaged in learning.

23. Homework—Young person reports doing at least one hour of homework every school day.

24. Bonding to school—Young person cares about her or his school.

25. Reading for pleasure—Young person reads for pleasure three or more hours per week.

Positive Values

26. Caring—Young person places high value on helping other people.

27. Equality and social justice—Young person places high value on promoting equality and reducing hunger and poverty.

28. Integrity—Young person acts on convictions and stands up for her or his beliefs.

29. Honesty—Young person "tells the truth even when it is not easy."

30. Responsibility—Young person accepts and takes personal responsibility.

31. Restraint—Young person believes it is important not to be sexually active or to use alcohol or other drugs.

Social Competencies

32. Planning and decision making—Young person knows how to plan ahead and make choices.

33. Interpersonal competence—Young person has empathy, sensitivity, and friendship skills.

34. Cultural competence—Young person has knowledge of and comfort with people of different cultural/racial/ethnic backgrounds.

35. Resistance skills—Young person can resist negative peer pressure and dangerous situations.

36. Peaceful conflict resolution—Young person seeks to resolve conflict nonviolently.

Positive Identity

37. Personal power—Young person feels he or she has control over "things that happen to me."

38. Self-esteem—Young person reports having a high self-esteem.

39. Sense of purpose—Young person reports that "my life has a purpose."

40. Positive view of personal future—Young person is optimistic about her or his personal future.

many others—can contribute to strengthening the asset foundation for children and youth.

At the core of asset building is Search Institute's research-based framework of 40 developmental assets (see Figure 5). The assets are grouped into two types: *external assets* refer to the support and opportunities that are provided by family, friends, organizations, and communities; *internal assets* focus on the capacities, skills, and values that develop within young people.

These assets aren't new ideas. They are the kinds of things parents, extended family, teachers, youth workers, neighbors, community leaders, and others have valued and offered for years—probably throughout history. Furthermore, they are grounded in many years of research in adolescent development, prevention, and resiliency.[5]

But while the assets represent experiences and qualities that most people want for young people, surveys of almost 100,000 6th- to 12th-grade youth in 213 communities across the United States show that most young people do not experience many of these assets. The average young person surveyed during the 1996–97 school year experiences only 18 of the 40. Furthermore, 63 percent of these youth experience 20 or fewer of the assets.[6] So while most people do not see these assets as anything new or remarkable, this society is not effective in ensuring that most or all young people have access to them in their lives.[7]

QUESTIONS TO CONSIDER

▶ How does the asset framework reinforce your past or current efforts and experiences in engaging young people in service or service-learning?

▶ What new perspective does the asset framework bring to you regarding service and service-learning?

However, young people from all backgrounds, economic levels, and ages who do experience the assets reap the benefits—as do the families, institutions, communities, and societies they live in. The more assets young people experience, the more likely they are to do well in school, contribute to their communities, take care of their health, and experience many other positive outcomes. Furthermore, the assets are also important factors in young people's choices about risky behaviors such as alcohol and other drug use. As young people's experiences of assets go up, their involvement in many different high-risk behaviors goes down, and they are more likely to exhibit indicators of thriving. (Table 1 illustrates these relationships.)

The Asset-Building Potential of Service-Learning

The power of assets in shaping young people's choices has motivated hundreds of communities and thousands of individuals and organizations to join in efforts to build developmental assets in and around children and youth. Many quickly recognize the potential for service-learning as a strategy toward that end.

Indeed, research and practice in the field of service-learning have found that engaging in service to others has clear potential for building assets. Search Institute researcher Peter C. Scales says that research shows service-learning contributing to asset building in three broad areas:

1. Building prosocial value and, to some extent, prosocial behavior;

2. Enhancing aspects of personal identity, such as self-esteem; and

3. Enhancing school success, such as grades and motivation in school.[8]

In addition, a Search Institute synthesis of the research on adolescent development identified a number of studies that point to the asset-building

TABLE 1

THE POWER OF DEVELOPMENTAL ASSETS

Thriving Behavior	Definition	0–10 Assets	11–20 Assets	21–30 Assets	31–40 Assets
Succeeds in School	Gets mostly A's on report card.	7%	19%	35%	53%
Values Diversity	Places high importance on getting to know people of other racial/ethnic groups.	34%	53%	69%	87%
Helps Others	Helps friends or neighbors one or more hours per week.	69%	83%	91%	96%
Exhibits Leadership	Has been a leader of a group or organization in the past 12 months.	48%	67%	78%	87%

Risk Behavior Pattern	Definition	0–10 Assets	11–20 Assets	21–30 Assets	31–40 Assets
Problem Alcohol Use	Has used alcohol three or more times in the past 30 days or got drunk once or more in the past two weeks.	53%	30%	11%	3%
Illicit Drug Use	Used illicit drugs (cocaine, LSD, PCP or angel dust, heroin, and amphetamines) three or more times in the past 12 months.	42%	19%	6%	1%
Sexual Activity	Has had sexual intercourse three or more times in lifetime.	33%	21%	10%	3%
Violence	Has engaged in three or more acts of fighting, hitting, injuring a person, carrying a weapon, or threatening physical harm in the past 12 months.	61%	35%	16%	6%

Based on a sample of almost 100,000 young people in 213 communities in 25 states who were surveyed during the 1996–97 school year.

potential of service-learning, community service, and volunteering. As shown in Figure 6, many of the outcomes that researchers have connected with service to others relate to six of the eight categories of assets in Search Institute's framework.

One effort that has examined service-learning's asset-building impact is the YMCA's Earth Service Corps (YESC), a teen leadership and service-learning program originally developed by the YMCA of Greater Seattle and now operating nationwide. The clubs focus on leadership development, environmental education, community involvement, volunteerism, and cross-cultural awareness. As part of their role as external evaluators for YESC, Search Institute researchers Thomas H. Berkas and Renee Vraa surveyed 273 youth in 33 YESC clubs in 1998. Figure 7 shows how these youth described their YESC experiences as they relate to each category of developmental assets.

Service-Learning as a Strategy for Culture Change

Another way to understand the connections between service-learning and asset building is to recognize that both approaches share similar strategies. In his book *All Kids Are Our Kids,* Search Institute

president Peter L. Benson, who created the asset framework, suggests that rebuilding the asset infrastructure for young people will require major culture change. He identifies 12 culture shifts, 10 of which are particularly relevant to service-learning:

1. A shift from deficit language to asset language— Instead of focusing on the problems in young people's lives, we need to shift energy to building the positive foundation for development that young people need to thrive.

2. A shift from some youth to all youth—While we must continue to pay special attention to those children who grow up in poverty and face other challenges, a critical task is to tap collective energy to build a solid foundation for all youth.

3. A shift from age segregation to intergenerational community—We need to shift from being a society in which young people have little meaningful contact with other generations to a society in which every young person has several sustained relationships with adults of all ages and with younger children.

4. A shift from a program focus to a relational focus—Most of the assets are built primarily through relationships with caring and responsible peers and adults. Rather than depending on programs and professionals to socialize young people, we must rediscover the power and centrality of relationships in passing on knowledge, wisdom, values, and priorities. It's critical that programs become a *supporting* cast, not the lead actors in caring for our children and youth.

5. A shift from a fragmented agenda to a unifying vision—If all socializing systems in a community share a commitment to a vision of healthy development, each can see its own niche in the larger vision. Everyone doesn't have to do everything, but all recognize that they are on the same team, working for the good of young people, rather than vying for attention for their particular agenda.

6. A shift from conflicting signals to consistent messages—Young people need to hear consistent mes-

FIGURE 6

SERVICE-LEARNING OUTCOMES CONNECTED TO ASSET BUILDING

In *Developmental Assets: A Synthesis of the Scientific Research on Adolescent Development* (pp. 56–57), Search Institute researchers Peter C. Scales and Nancy Leffert identify numerous positive outcomes of service-learning, volunteering, and community service during adolescence. Although results vary widely, depending on the intensity and quality of service-learning studied, researchers frequently have found that many things increase, to a greater or lesser degree, for young people engaging in service to others.

SUPPORT

▶ Positive attitudes toward adults

▶ Talking with parents about school

EMPOWERMENT

▶ Community involvement

▶ Political participation and interest

▶ Positive attitudes toward community involvement

▶ Positive civic attitudes

▶ Belief that one can make a difference in community

▶ Leadership positions in community organizations

COMMITMENT TO LEARNING

▶ Grades in reading

▶ School attendance and performance

▶ Commitment to class work

▶ Working for good grades

POSITIVE VALUES

▶ Prosocial and moral reasoning

▶ Empathy

▶ Personal and social responsibility

▶ Perceived duty to help others

▶ Altruism

▶ Concern for others' welfare

▶ Awareness of societal problems

SOCIAL COMPETENCIES

▶ Self-disclosure

▶ Development of mature relationships

▶ Social competence outside of school

▶ Problem-solving skills

POSITIVE IDENTITY

▶ Self-concept

▶ Self-esteem

▶ Self-efficacy

FIGURE 7

YOUNG PEOPLE'S ASSET-BUILDING EXPERIENCES IN A SERVICE-LEARNING PROGRAM

Search Institute surveys of 273 youth in 33 YMCA Earth Service Corps (YESC) clubs show many ways in which the experience can help build young people's assets. Here are the percentages of young people who agreed or strongly agreed with each statement regarding their YESC club, organized by seven of the eight categories of developmental assets.* (These statements are not the developmental assets themselves, but rather the kinds of experiences that contribute to asset building.)

SUPPORT

Club advisers listen to me.	94%
Club advisers make me feel like I belong.	93%
Other club members care about me.	90%
I could go to a club adviser for advice on a serious problem.	75%

EMPOWERMENT

In club activities, I am given a chance to help.	94%
Club advisers make me feel important.	89%

BOUNDARIES AND EXPECTATIONS

In club activities, adults expect the best from me.	96%
Club advisers challenge me to do my best.	87%

COMMITMENT TO LEARNING

Being in YESC makes me want to learn more about new things.	89%
Club advisers encourage me to do well in school.	78%
Participation in the club has made me want to try harder in school.	70%

POSITIVE VALUES *(Being in YESC has made these values more important.)*

Being responsible for what I do.	98%
Caring about other people.	96%
Standing up for what I believe, even when it's not popular to do so.	95%
Telling the truth, even when it's not easy.	93%

SOCIAL COMPETENCIES

Club activities have helped me get along with others.	88%
Club activities have helped me make better decisions.	81%
Club activities have helped me make and keep friends.	80%

POSITIVE IDENTITY

Club activities have helped me learn what I do does make a difference.	94%
Club activities have helped me get a better sense of what I can do.	91%
Club activities have helped me feel good about myself.	86%
Club activities have helped me realize I have a lot to be proud of.	83%

*Thomas H. Berkas and Renee Vraa, "YMCA Earth Service Corps: Phase II, July 1997–June 1998" (unpublished report, Search Institute, 1998), 22–29.

sages about what society expects of them. These messages include a commitment to core human values such as honesty, caring, compassion, and justice. Yet young people today hear many signals that erode positive, shared social commitments. Many of these conflicting signals grow out of a dominant culture that emphasizes self-interest, consumerism, and competition, often to the detriment of values of concern for others, sharing, and cooperation.

7. A shift from efficiency only to intentional redundancy—Raising children is not an efficient process, and relationships are not efficient. Young people need to be exposed to asset-building opportunities over and over in all parts of their lives.

8. A shift from youth as objects to youth as actors—John P. Kretzmann and Paul H. Schmitz capture this society's conventional wisdom about young people's role: "In the cliché, people (adults) in villages act to 'raise' young people. Young folks are the objects of the action, never the subjects. They are defined as deficient—of knowledge, of skills, of any useful capacities—and relegated with their cohorts to the filling stations we call schools. The assumption is that, magically, at age 18 or 21, young people will emerge from their years of being filled, and re-enter the community as full and useful contributors."

YOUTH VOICE

RASHEED NEWSON,
SOPHOMORE, GEORGETOWN
UNIVERSITY, WASHINGTON, D.C.

"One reason youth volunteer is because, at their best, volunteer opportunities allow youth to be in control, to make decisions. Unfortunately, the lives of youth don't allow them that kind of freedom. They go to school as they're told and shuffle from classroom to classroom at the sounding of a bell. How often does anyone go to them with major decisions and say, 'What do you think we should do?' "[9]

This perspective, Kretzmann and Schmitz suggest, "is a disaster. Not only has it produced a generation of young people who think of themselves as useless, but it has isolated that generation from productive interaction with older generations. It has relegated more than a third of our citizens to inaction or worse and has deprived our youth of the experience necessary for fulfilling their roles as citizens and contributors to the community."[10]

9. A shift from changing priorities to long-term commitment—The developmental assets provide a framework for long-term action that recognizes the importance of ongoing, positive opportunities and relationships.

10. A shift from civic disengagement to engagement—Asset building calls for people to get involved in the public life of the community, reconnecting with those around them in relationships of mutual support, care, and shared responsibility.[11]

Thus, asset building begins with a set of experiences and attributes that young people need in their lives to thrive (though most young people don't have enough of them). Rebuilding that foundation requires that everyone discover their potential and opportunities for building assets. It also calls for institutions and programs that support young people to find ways to ensure that their efforts contribute as much as possible to strengthening young people's asset foundation.

These ten culture shifts point to the many things that service-learning has to offer the asset-building movement. Since its inception, the service-learning movement has emphasized a positive understanding of young people, engagement of all youth, youth as actors and contributors, and nurturing ongoing engagement in civic and community life.

Other themes in asset building clearly resonate with service-learning and are often emphasized in specific programs. For example, many service-learning efforts focus on building intergenerational relationships and understanding.

In addition, the asset-building vision reminds service-learning proponents not to lose sight of their role in the multifaceted task of raising healthy children and youth. For example:

■ The emphasis on intergenerational community encourages service-learning programs to develop service-learning experiences that engage children, youth, parents, and other adults side by side in serving and learning together.

■ The emphasis on relationships reminds leaders that service-learning programs are means to an end, not ends in themselves.

■ The emphasis on intentional redundancy calls for recognizing, celebrating, and linking with the many diverse opportunities young people have to serve others and contribute to their communities. Instead of competing for young people's participation, this perspective seeks to acknowledge and support all who engage young people in service, whether through their family, school, congregation, youth organization, social service agency, or with a group of peers who band together to address a shared concern.

■ Service-learning can contribute to consistent messages as proponents seek to make a commitment to serving others a norm in the community. That message is particularly powerful when people of all ages—from young children to senior citizens—participate side by side in contributing to the community and serving others.

Finally, the shift to a long-term perspective recognizes that a service-learning program cannot, on

its own or in a few weeks, nurture in young people a lasting commitment to service, caring, and "the common good." These deep commitments grow out of many relationships and experiences, beginning in early childhood and continuing through adolescence and adulthood.

What Asset Building Offers Service-Learning

It is clear that service-learning has great potential as an asset-building strategy. Indeed, an effective service-learning program does not even have to be aware of developmental assets to have a profound impact on young people's lives.

At the same time, it is helpful to examine how an asset-building perspective can challenge and strengthen service-learning as well. Put another way, what does asset building add to an already effective service-learning effort? We suggest that there are seven perspectives that an asset-building approach can bring to service-learning. And while many service-learning programs may already have these perspectives, the asset framework reinforces and articulates them in a new way.

1. A relational perspective—At its core, asset building is about relationship building. As important as the tasks or action being undertaken through service-learning experiences are, it is also critical to recognize the relational dimension to serving others—relationships with coworkers, those being served, parents and other adults, and adult program leaders. It is through relationships that young people often first get involved in service, and it is often the relationships that keep them committed.

2. An additive perspective—Quality service-learning can happen in a single, isolated program. But an asset-building lens encourages us to remember the value of multiple exposures to service over time in a wide variety of contexts throughout childhood and adolescence, with one experience building on and

QUESTIONS TO CONSIDER

▶ Which culture shifts seem most important to you? Which ones, if any, seem unimportant?

▶ Does thinking of service-learning as a strategy for culture change alter your understanding of service-learning and its importance? How?

reinforcing the other. From this perspective, each service-learning program recognizes, affirms, and supports others who engage young people in service, knowing that each is part of a larger vision of making service and civic engagement a norm for all children, youth, and adults.

3. A developmental perspective—Asset building doesn't begin in adolescence. Neither does a commitment to serving others and contributing to the world. Young people begin forming their commitments and values early in life, and those priorities continue to be reinforced (or challenged) as they move through adolescence toward adulthood. Thus, asset building suggests the importance of engaging young people in service beginning at early ages, then reinforcing and building on those experienced through adolescence.

Research supports the importance of a developmental perspective on service-learning. Independent Sector studies of volunteering among youth and adults consistently find that children who volunteer are more likely to serve as teenagers.[12] Furthermore, teenagers who volunteer are more likely to serve as adults.[13] Thus, we will be more effective in getting young people into the "habit" of serving others, if we recognize and plan for ongoing, repeated opportunities to volunteer and contribute throughout childhood and adolescence.

4. A multisector perspective—Young people get involved in serving others through many places in their communities. As Figure 8 shows, young people first get involved primarily through their congregations and schools, and, to a lesser extent, youth organizations and community groups.

However, rarely are these parallel and compatible efforts recognized, linked, or cross-pollinated. In most cases, one organization in a community develops its own service-learning experiences in isolation from others. A school, congregation, or youth organization may link with a social service agency to identify specific projects. But most communities miss the value and potential of having various service-learning efforts learn from each other, coordinate activities, and provide mutual support—not to mention the value of the redundant, consistent message that such cooperation sends to young people.

Youth development specialists Shepherd Zeldin and Suzanne Tarlov put the challenge this way: "It is unfortunate . . . that information gaps and suspicions too often characterize relationships among schools and community organizations. Neither the school nor the community organizations have the resources to provide high-quality service learning for all young people. Ongoing communication and collaboration, therefore, are necessary. The challenge is to bridge the gaps between organizations that have a similar mission."[14] Adding to the challenge, Zeldin and Tarlov focus only on bringing together

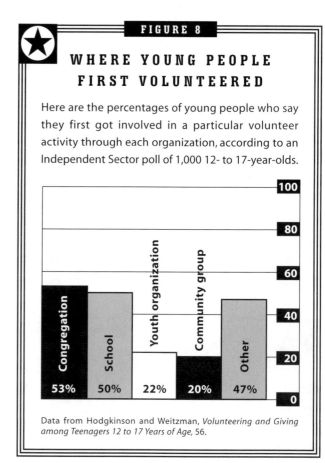

FIGURE 8

WHERE YOUNG PEOPLE FIRST VOLUNTEERED

Here are the percentages of young people who say they first got involved in a particular volunteer activity through each organization, according to an Independent Sector poll of 1,000 12- to 17-year-olds.

Congregation 53%
School 50%
Youth organization 22%
Community group 20%
Other 47%

Data from Hodgkinson and Weitzman, *Volunteering and Giving among Teenagers 12 to 17 Years of Age,* 56.

youth development organizations and schools. A greater challenge is also to connect the religious community, particularly since the suspicion of the religious community can be quite strong in other sectors, and vice versa.

5. A holistic perspective—"Service to others" is one of the 40 developmental assets. But the asset-building framework offers many other connections to service-learning. Indeed, a service-learning experience intentionally can address many of the assets in many categories, giving the experience a well-rounded, holistic grounding.

Table 2 suggests some connections between service-learning and each of the eight categories of developmental assets. In this way, the asset framework becomes a lens for examining service-learning activities. You can ask whether the activity not only teaches a subject and provides a service but also reinforces positive values, deepens a commitment to learning, and gives a sense of purpose and power to everyone involved.

6. A strength-building perspective—An asset-building perspective highlights the importance of building assets not only with young servers but also among those being served. Thus, asset-based service-learning seeks to tap their strengths, form positive relationships, offer empowering help, and strengthen the opportunities for growth, development, and support.

The asset-building perspective shaped the service project initiated by Brian Elkins, a 9th grader at Colorado Academy in southwest Denver. When Brian heard about developmental assets, he believed the framework offered a great opportunity to fulfill his community service requirement for graduation. So he worked with his teacher and 11 classmates to identify a project that would integrate the assets with service. They ended up painting a mural at the Catholic Charities Mulroy Neighborhood Center. "Each part of the mural shows what parents can do to sup-

QUESTIONS TO CONSIDER

▶ Which of the seven perspectives outlined has the most potential for helping to strengthen service or service-learning efforts in which you are engaged?

▶ What other ways, if any, have you found that an asset-building lens refocuses your service or service-learning efforts?

▶ What do you see as the benefits and challenges of building bridges between asset building and service-learning?

port their children," he says. "Share, smile a lot, be proud of their work, and read to them." The positive messages inspired by asset building have left a lasting mark on the neighborhood center.

7. A "laboratory" perspective—If one primary aim of service-learning is to nurture a commitment to serving others and contributing to the common good, then it is important to remember that service-learning experiences are only one of the factors that shape these commitments. Many other influences also shape young people's commitment to serving. Some of these include:

■ Early experiences of being loved and cared for;

■ Community and family role models of service;

■ Ongoing, daily expectations to be generous, share, and "help out"; and

■ Personal and religious values and beliefs.

Service-learning experiences are the laboratory or training ground for a life of serving others. They are where you practice, learn the skills, and have lots of support to do it. But no team spends all its time on the practice field. It's also important to go out and play the game in "real life."

This point in no way diminishes the value of service-learning. Indeed, the concrete experience of serving others—and then reflecting on that experi-

TABLE 2

SERVICE-LEARNING CONNECTIONS TO THE EIGHT CATEGORIES OF DEVELOPMENTAL ASSETS

Asset Category	Description	Service-Learning Connections
1. Support	Young people need to experience care, love, and involvement from their family, neighbors, and many others. They need organizations and institutions that provide positive, supportive environments.	Working together on service-learning projects can cement relationships of support and caring between peers and with parents and other adults.
2. Empowerment	Young people need to be valued by their community and have opportunities to contribute to others. For this to occur, they must feel safe.	As they contribute to their world, young people become experts about issues that are important to them, and are seen and see themselves as valuable resources for their organizations and communities. Careful preparation and good supervision during their service-learning efforts help them feel safe.
3. Boundaries and expectations	Young people need to know what is expected of them and whether behaviors are "in bounds" or "out of bounds."	Boundaries and expectations are reinforced when activities include ground rules for involvement and as adults and peers become positive role models for each other.
4. Constructive use of time	Young people need constructive, enriching opportunities for growth through creative activities, youth programs, involvement with a center of worship or spirituality, and quality time at home.	Service-learning provides opportunities for young people to use their time to expand their minds and hearts, offer hope and support to others, and use their creativity to deal with new challenges and opportunities.
5. Commitment to learning	Young people need to develop a lifelong commitment to education and learning.	Education linked to action can unleash a new commitment to learning as youth apply their knowledge to issues and problems and as they are exposed to questions and situations that challenge their worldview and perspectives.
6. Positive values	Young people need to develop strong values that guide their choices.	Through service learning, young people not only express their positive values, they also have opportunities to affirm and internalize values that are important to them.
7. Social competencies	Young people need skills and competencies that equip them to make positive choices, to build relationships, and to succeed in life.	Many skills and social competencies are nurtured as young people plan their activities, take action, and build relationships with their peers, adults who serve with them, and service recipients.
8. Positive identity	Young people need a strong sense of their own purpose, power, and promise.	Service-learning becomes an important catalyst for shaping positive identity as young people discover their gifts and a place in the world through their acts of service and justice.

ence—plays a critical role in solidifying and deepening a commitment to caring and to the common good. Princeton University's Robert Wuthnow puts it this way: "Volunteering is the route by which young people move from a primordial understanding of caring—rooted in family ties—to a more specialized understanding that will serve them better as they assume responsibilities in complex social institutions. Volunteering is thus an important link between having good intentions and being able to put them into practice."[15]

Putting the Connections to Work

This chapter has focused on identifying the connections between asset building and service-learning. We have tried to make the case that service-learning can strengthen asset-building efforts *and* that asset building can strengthen service-learning efforts. To take advantage of this opportunity, though, it is important to build a solid foundation for service-learning. The next three chapters focus on various issues in laying that foundation.

CHAPTER 2

CULTIVATING LEADERSHIP
AND SUPPORT

Service-learning is most effective when it is an ongoing, sustained part of an organization's programming. In schools, this means that it becomes an integral part of the curriculum. In congregations and youth organizations, it means that service-learning is a regular part of programming, not just something that happens every once in a while.

So while you may be able to pull off a service project here and there on your own, you'll have far more impact if you work to gain wide support for an *ongoing* commitment to service-learning. The Alliance for Service-Learning in Education Reform puts the issue this way:

> *In order for service-learning to be accepted and succeed in any setting, it must receive institutional support for its philosophy and financial requirements. School-based service-learning needs the support of both district and building administrators. Too often, educators enthusiastic about service-learning are offered token support, largely in words of praise for "wonderful work" that is being accomplished.[1]*

This chapter focuses on key elements of gaining support within your school, congregation, or other organization as well as the community.

Identify a Champion/Coordinator

To be most effective, a service-learning effort needs one person—a coordinator or champion—who makes sure things happen and who keeps moving forward in spite of the inevitable barriers that arise. "The new idea or practice either finds a champion or dies," writes Bruce Joyce. "No ordinary involvement with a new idea produces the energy to cope with indifference and resistance that major change provokes."[2]

Some of the things a coordinator or champion does include:

- Articulating the vision of asset building and the potential young people have to make a difference in the world;
- Uniting people around a shared commitment to service-learning and asset building;
- Ensuring that the needed tools and resources are available so that things run smoothly;
- Networking other asset builders on behalf of young people; and
- Being an advocate and ally for young people and their power to make a difference.

A coordinator's job is *not* to do everything that needs to be done. Trying to control everything can actually undermine the power and potential of service-learning to develop young people's skills and sense of accomplishment. Sharing responsibility and authority for virtually every dimension of planning is critical to the success of your effort. It also becomes an important part of the growth and learning for the others involved.

A Points of Light Foundation resource on service-learning for community agencies has identified six characteristics of an effective service-learning champion; these same characteristics apply to service-learning champions in other settings as well. A service-learning champion:

1. Believes in the capabilities of children and teen-agers;

2. Sees the vision and potential of service-learning in the organization;

3. Can articulate the vision and how it could enhance the organization's mission;

4. Has credibility, positive relationships, and an ability to motivate others within the organization;

5. Understands the dynamics, concerns, and needs of the organization; and

6. Is flexible and open to new possibilities.[3]

Build a Core Leadership Group

Effective service-learning efforts have a team of 6 to 12 leaders who design and implement service-learning activities. Having a mixture of people on this team adds credibility to your efforts, builds youth buy-in early on, sends the message that parental support is key to the success of your efforts, provides a forum for different concerns to be raised and addressed, and more evenly distributes the workload.

There are at least three groups to involve in leadership. Use Worksheet 1 to identify and follow up with potential leaders.

Youth leaders—No service-learning effort should be planned and led just by adults. Having young people in leadership roles is key to the success of any service-learning. Young people who invest their time and energy into planning and leading throughout the process will be more engaged and more com-

mitted to the work you are doing. In addition, their involvement in leading builds their own assets as they take on useful roles (asset #8: youth as resources), develop plans (asset #32: planning and decision making), and engage in many other activities that relate directly to many of the assets.

In identifying young people for leadership roles, keep in mind the many different types of young people who can contribute—not just the outgoing, visible leaders. A quiet boy may be the kind of leader who listens well, puts ideas together, and helps see things in new ways. An energetic girl may have just the right personality to coordinate supplies and schedules. Most young people have gifts to be tapped for leadership.[4]

Adult allies—In the same way that young people are critical, it's also important to have adults actively involved in planning and leading—to be allies for the young people. Adults can bring important perspectives, knowledge, experience, skills, and connections with them to the table. Not only can they work with young people to accomplish the tasks, they also form relationships with the young people. Those relationships become the opportunity for

> **YOUTH VOICE**
>
> ### BECKY JARVIS
> **SENIOR, ST. PAUL ACADEMY,**
> **ST. PAUL, MINNESOTA**
>
> "As a youth representative, it is empowering to see adults and their organizations making solid investments in my future and also in my present. But it is even more empowering to work with adults to make that investment for myself. When youth take ownership—when human beings take ownership —we take more responsibility and pride in the policies we set and in the programs we create. It is this personal responsibility and pride that build our communities and make them strong."[5]

IDENTIFYING POSSIBLE LEADERS FOR SERVICE-LEARNING

Use this worksheet to identify people who can fill different roles. List people's names in the middle column. Then, in the right column, keep notes about their particular qualities, gifts, interests, and knowledge that could strengthen your service-learning efforts.

Role	Possible People	Qualities, Gifts, Interests, and Knowledge They Bring
Coordinator		
Youth Leaders		
Adult Allies		
Community Partners		

building many assets, including other adult relationships (asset #3), community values youth (asset #7), and adult role models (asset #14).

Some potential adult allies include:

- Youth leaders;
- Parents;
- Community adults who care about youth and asset building;
- Community activists who are committed to passing on traditions of service and justice to young people;
- Members of your organization's leadership; and
- Other people in your organization who have experience with service or service-learning.

In some ways, an ally's formal roles are less important than her or his attitude toward youth. "Adults as allies recognize youth as valuable resources with a right and responsibility to serve the community," writes Barry Checkoway of the University of Michigan. "They help bring people together, provide resources for activities, deal with bureaucracies, and overcome the obstacles. They respect your ideas, give group encouragement, and build mutual support."[6]

A commitment to asset building challenges you to look beyond the obvious places to identify adult allies. Often we assume that those allies will be parents of youth or young adults who are "a lot like the kids." While both parents and young adults certainly can be great allies, asset building recognizes that all responsible adults have something to offer young people. Some of the best allies may be retired community members who see a bit of themselves in the young people and are eager to share their passions, commitments, and wisdom with the young leaders. Others may be childless adults who thoroughly enjoy the energy and potential of young people and who have a passion for service and justice.

Community partners—One of the principles of effective service-learning is that the community is actively engaged in shaping the service projects. Otherwise, young people may have a good time and

> **QUESTIONS TO CONSIDER**
>
> ▶ How would you describe the current leadership of service or service-learning efforts in your organization? Do one or two people do it all? Or are many people involved?
>
> ▶ From your perspective, what are the benefits and challenges of engaging a wide variety of people in leadership roles? How might you address some of the challenges?
>
> ▶ What concerns do you have about involving youth in leadership? What can you do to deal with your concerns and make youth leadership a good experience for all?

learn a lot, but their efforts may not actually benefit the community, or, worse yet, they create a sense of disempowerment and paternalism. Indeed, a frequent critique of youth service projects is that they're designed to meet the needs and interests of the young people but not the needs and priorities of the community or those being served.

One way to address this concern is to invite community members to be part of the leadership for your service-learning efforts so that they have an active say in how the program is designed. In addition, they can help introduce young people to the real issues in the community and begin to overcome stereotypes or misperceptions that might otherwise shape the planning.

Another type of community partner to include would be the agencies and organizations in a community that already offer services. Too often, schools, congregations, or youth organizations invest a great deal of time and energy designing a project that someone else in the community already does and does well. Imagine how much more could be done and learned if the organizations serving youth actively partnered with the organizations addressing community needs to design service-learning projects together!

Such a partnership contributes to the asset-building vision in which many sectors of a community connect with each other and work together on behalf of young people. This cooperation not only allows for better use of resources, it also opens possibilities for more service opportunities for youth as well as strengthened relationships in the community.

Shape a Vision Grounded in the Organization's Mission and Identity

As suggested in Chapter 1, asset-based service-learning can have a positive impact on the young people, the organization, the recipients of the service, and the larger community. In addition, there are clear connections to the mission, purpose, and priorities of many different kinds of organizations, as shown in Figure 9.

From another perspective, Novella Zett Keith of Temple University notes that service-learning can connect to three areas of school life that have parallels in other settings:

1. Instruction—Service-learning offers a hands-on alternative approach to learning that emphasizes cooperative learning and multiple opportunities for success.

2. Curriculum—Service-learning can guide the development of meaningful, relevant curriculum tied to local realities and knowledge.

3. Community building and development—Service-learning enhances relationships within the school (or other organization), as well as school-community relationships. Programs, Keith writes, "should have as their express goals the building of 'two-way bridges' across the bounds of diversity, facilitating cross-cultural understanding, relationship building, and the creation of communities of support."[7]

These general benefits and opportunities can provide a foundation for discussion and planning. In addition, your leadership group and organization need to grapple with how service-learning and asset building tie specifically to your organization's mission and values, history and experience, and readiness and capacity. Examining these connections helps:

■ Clarify why your organization is engaging in asset-based service-learning;

■ Gain buy-in from organizational leaders and decision makers;

■ Shape your programming to fit your organization's character, priorities, and strengths;

■ Diffuse resistance (if you can show that what you're doing is similar to something the organization did 50 years ago, it's harder for naysayers to complain that "we've never done it this way before");

■ Determine how to get started or what to do next; and

■ Identify potential obstacles and barriers.

Worksheet 2 lists a series of questions that may be useful in identifying connections to your organization's mission, history, and readiness. These kinds of questions lead to the vision you have for asset-based service-learning in your school, congregation, youth organization, or other setting. A vision gives you a sense of what kind of difference this effort will make. What will people see, feel, hear, or touch that's different because of the investment in this effort? How will young people feel about themselves and their community? How will the organization be

---

? QUESTIONS TO CONSIDER

▶ What do you see as the strongest links between asset-based service-learning and your organization's mission and identity? How can you build on those strengths?

▶ What is your vision for service-learning in your organization? How widely is that vision shared?

▶ What can you do to bring alive the vision of service-learning within your organization?

FIGURE 9

SOME CONNECTIONS BETWEEN ASSET-BASED SERVICE-LEARNING AND THE MISSIONS OF DIFFERENT ORGANIZATIONS

Service-Learning Offers Schools:

◗ A student-centered experiential learning method that connects classroom teaching with real-world issues and realities;

◗ A methodology that, if done well, can increase school success in areas such as higher grades and motivation in school;

◗ A strategy for working toward schools' citizenship goals and priorities;

◗ A vehicle for school reform; and

◗ An opportunity to build partnerships with the community.

Service-Learning Offers Youth-Serving Organizations:

◗ A link between two common mission areas: service or citizenship, and healthy development of children and youth;

◗ A powerful, life-shaping experience for vulnerable young people as they recognize their own capacity to lead and contribute; and

◗ Concrete, meaningful activities for program participants.

Service-Learning Offers Congregations:

◗ A powerful strategy for living out a central tenet or belief of every major world religion;

◗ A way to give young people opportunities to put their faith into practice while also shaping their attitudes and beliefs;

◗ A strategy for cultivating leaders for the congregation and the faith community; and

◗ A way to keep young people connected to the congregation and their faith.

Service-Learning Offers Community-Based Service Agencies:

◗ Added resources and capacity for meeting the organization's mission, whether it is providing direct services to people in need, advocating for particular causes, or educating the public;

◗ Opportunities for community residents served by agencies to interact with young people;

◗ The energy and excitement young people often bring; and

◗ The beginnings of a long-term commitment by young people to address particular issues and to be active in the community.

Service-Learning Offers Community-Wide Asset-Building Initiatives:

◗ A concrete activity around which many sectors of the community work together;

◗ A focal point for recognizing young people as resources for the community; and

◗ Projects that attract the community's attention and interest.

FINDING CONNECTIONS BETWEEN ASSET-BASED SERVICE-LEARNING AND YOUR ORGANIZATION'S MISSION, HISTORY, AND READINESS

Use the following questions to guide conversations with your leadership group and others in your organization about how asset-based service-learning fits in your organization or initiative. Refer to Chapter 1 to identify some possible connections.

Mission and Values

▶ What is the mission of your organization? How can asset-based service-learning enhance and contribute to that mission?

▶ Does your organization have strategic priorities or goals that connect to asset building and service-learning?

▶ What are the foundational theories, philosophies, or beliefs in your organization that tie to asset building and service-learning? (For example, a school may have a philosophy of education that emphasizes student-centered learning about real-world issues. A youth organization may have a founder who was committed to youth empowerment. Or a congregation may point to important beliefs, sacred writings, or teachings that urge a commitment to serving others.)

▶ What values of your organization relate to asset building or service-learning? How can your service-learning efforts focus on strengthening those values?

▶ Are there parts of your organization's mission or values that might clash with an emphasis on asset-based service-learning? If so, how can you address those areas?

History and Experience

▶ Can you identify in the history of your organization specific activities, emphases, and commitments that tie to service-learning? (For example, does everyone still talk about the highly successful canned food drive of 10 years ago?)

▶ What kinds of service, volunteering, social action, or experiential education already occur in your organization (even if youth are not involved)? How can these experiences be built upon to show the value and place of asset-based service-learning?

▶ Do people talk about any failed experiences that could become roadblocks to asset-based service-learning? How will you show how your new efforts will be different from—and learn from—past mistakes?

Readiness and Capacity

▶ How will you design your asset-based service-learning efforts so that they are not overambitious for your organization's previous experience? (If your organization doesn't have any history of getting youth to volunteer or serve others, you'll most likely be successful if you start small.)

▶ Do you have a group of people (including young people) within the organization who are committed to planning, leading, and guiding your effort?

▶ Are young people already viewed as resources within your organization? If not, how will you work on changing perceptions of young people?

viewed differently? Answering those kinds of questions, even informally, begins to help you and your organization develop a passion and commitment to asset-based service-learning.

There are many ways to make this vision and possibility come alive for people. Three of these possibilities are:

■ Sponsoring short-term experiments or trial runs in which a few young people engage in service-learning so that people can see the early successes;

■ Making site visits to similar organizations that have engaged young people in service-learning; and

■ Sharing success stories from other places.

Connect Service-Learning to Existing Programs and Activities

Most organizations already have too much to do. Schools have long lists of curriculum requirements. Youth organizations and congregations have limited time with young people, and they, too, have much they want to accomplish in those few hours. So while there are appropriate ways to add new service-learning activities and programs to an organization, it's even more effective to connect service-learning to something that is already happening—something with a core of support and ongoing commitment.

In schools, service-learning can be integrated into the core curriculum as a learning strategy for many subject areas. By making service-learning a core teaching strategy, you don't add programming or expand the curriculum per se; rather, service-

learning becomes a strategy for reaching an existing goal or priority. For example, doing a service-learning project to address prejudice or racism can open the doors for a relevant and engaging study of the civil rights movement in a history or social studies class.

Similarly, youth organizations and congregations can integrate service-learning into existing activities. A leadership development program in a youth organization could become a natural opportunity for service-learning. More and more congregations are making service-learning an integral part of the expectations for rites of passage such as confirmation or Bar/Bat Mitzvah. Others successfully integrate a service-learning component into established youth trips and summer events.

Gain Support from the Organization's Leadership

Rarely can efforts within organization be sustained without the support of leaders. In schools, these leaders might include the principal, school board, site council, and other decision makers. In youth organizations, it may be the executive director and board. In a congregation, it may be the senior clergy and the congregation's board.

These key leaders can play important roles in your efforts. Sometimes the organization's leaders will want to be an active part of the core service-learning team. More often, however, they will play other important roles, such as:

■ Sharing with others their support and enthusiasm for asset-based service-learning;

■ Making time for the coordinator and leadership group to plan and implement the service-learning effort;

■ Providing financial and material resources;

■ Encouraging people to participate (and dealing with any detractors);

■ Making connections to the community;

? QUESTIONS TO CONSIDER

> ▶ What leaders in your organization do you expect to be most supportive? Who do you expect will be the least supportive?
>
> ▶ In your experience, what kinds of information are most helpful to your organization's leadership in determining whether and how to support a new idea?
>
> ▶ What aspects of service-learning do you expect to have the most appeal to leaders? How can you most effectively highlight those aspects?

■ Helping spread the approach to other settings within and beyond the organization;

■ Ensuring that the service-learning efforts are consistent with the organization's policies, including risk management, liability, and transportation issues; and

■ Recognizing and celebrating service-learning efforts.

The best way to gain the support of key leaders is through one-on-one contacts and relationship building. In addition, you can use information you develop about how service-learning ties to your mission to make your case. It's important to seek advice throughout the process, rather than waiting until everything has been planned to talk with leaders about the effort.

Seek Support from Other Stakeholders

In addition to the leadership, it's important to have widespread support from stakeholders at all levels throughout the organization. Having broad buy-in creates energy and excitement for your service-learning efforts. It also opens up new possibilities and more people become interested and involved. And it helps sustain momentum and deflect any detractors.

Many different groups can have a stake in your service-learning efforts. These may include young people, teachers, other staff, parents, and the organization's constituency. Young people will clearly be affected if they are asked (or required) to participate in service-learning experiences. Parents have a stake in what kinds of experiences and education their children are participating in. Organization staff members may have a stake in whether a commitment to service-learning increases or changes their workload. The constituency served by a community agency has a stake in who provides services and how. Worksheet 3 helps you identify what kind of information you need to gather from and share with various stakeholders as you plan your service-learning efforts.

Some ways to get buy-in and support from various stakeholders include:

■ Telling people about developmental assets and their power in young people's lives;

■ Having young people carry the message and the vision, when possible;

■ Sharing the vision through informal conversations and formal presentations;

■ Asking for stakeholders' advice, ideas, and concerns;

■ Inviting them to participate in ways that interest them;

■ Listening sincerely to their concerns and doing what you can to address them;

? QUESTIONS TO CONSIDER

> ▶ What stakeholders in your organization need to be included in conversations about service-learning?
>
> ▶ What kinds of resistance do you expect from any of these people or groups? How can you prepare for that resistance?
>
> ▶ What kinds of resources might each person or group bring to your service-learning efforts? How can you invite people to offer these resources?

CONNECTING WITH STAKEHOLDERS

Use this worksheet to identify what to learn from and communicate to various stakeholders in your organization. Use the right-hand column to identify ways to connect with each group. This might include naming a person who has the most access or understanding of the group to be the point person.

	What You Need to Learn from Them	What You Need to Communicate to Them	How You Will Connect with Them
Young people			
Staff members			
Teachers/Leaders			
Parents			
The organization's constituency (people it serves, member-ship, etc.)			
Others			

- Posting information about the effort in appropriate places;
- Hosting events where stakeholders can see service-learning in action; and
- Connecting what you're doing to their areas of interest and passion.

Strategize for Long-Term Change

As is the case with any innovation or new approach, integrating service-learning into your organization is a long-term, challenging process. People often resist change, and often there are major bureaucratic challenges to overcome for an innovative idea to be accepted. It takes time to assess and plan, time that is in short supply for most program leaders.

The book *Combining Service and Learning* identifies a number of strategies for institutional and organizational change. They include:

- Being clear about where you want to go;
- Getting bottom-up support;
- Using changes in the organization or community as opportunities to introduce new ideas;
- Measuring what you want people to notice;
- Planning incremental, not sweeping, changes;
- Using outside funding to get something started;
- Being flexible and adjusting as you go;

- Expecting and responding to resistance;
- Telling people about your success; and
- Having rituals and ceremonies to mark progress.[8]

It can be hard to be patient through this change process. After all, you and the other service-learning champions are eager to see your efforts come to fruition. It's important to pace yourself so that you don't burn out or lose interest before reaching your goal. Longtime service-learning advocate Kate McPherson describes the challenge this way:

When we have a vision or sense of urgency about an issue, we tend to want to see it happen now. We don't very often have faith in the ebb and flow. We barely plant the flowers and then we keep pulling them up to see if they are growing. Instead, we need to allow them time to grow, to trust the ebb and flow and changes, and to honor the fact that different people's lives have seasons where they can give more or less attention to such an effort. If you have a commitment, make sure that you see how to integrate that commitment into your own quality of life so that you too can sustain it over time. Constant, steady pressure has more overall force and effect than an occasional, frantic shove.[9]

CHAPTER 3

MAKING SERVICE-LEARNING WORK
FOR ALL KIDS

"Everybody can be great because everybody can serve."
— Martin Luther King Jr.

All kids—regardless of physical, emotional, or intellectual abilities—can benefit from service-learning. Indeed, the wider the range of young people who are engaged in service and service-learning experiences, the greater the creativity and possibilities, as you match the unique gifts, talents, interests, experiences, and abilities of those involved with the needs and opportunities for service in the community. Consider these examples:

■ Young people in Connecticut join with adults in their community to raise awareness about the results of Search Institute's *Profiles of Student Life: Attitudes and Behaviors* survey. They plan a town meeting and create an inspirational video about what kids in their community need to succeed.[1]

■ Participants in Danville, California's Community Services Group—many of whom don't participate in traditional youth activities—turn the idea of a youth center inside out. They take on projects that benefit youth in the community, including running a coffee shop, planning concerts and dances, baby-sitting at a women's shelter, and helping younger kids plan fun activities.[2]

■ Fifth graders in Marquette, Michigan, learn math, science, and life skills in a unique way. They bake bread twice a month and deliver it to a local transitional residence for homeless people.

■ Police and church members in northern Minnesota collaborate to mentor first-time juvenile offenders in basic carpentry skills. The young people use what they learn to build picnic tables for the church—and relationships with their mentors.[3]

■ Youth Ventures gives grant money to young people to provide a number of needed services in their communities, including developing bilingual workbooks and audio tapes that encourage Spanish-speaking parents and children to work together to preserve their Spanish skills and build English proficiency.[4]

Each of these examples points to the wide variety of ways to engage young people in asset building. In addition, a focus on asset building reminds us of the potential for intergenerational service and family service. These groups open up additional opportunities and challenges.

The question, then, is not whether service-learning is appropriate for a particular group. The question is how to make service-learning developmentally responsive to the young people involved so that it can work well. This chapter looks at some of the specific ways service-learning can be applied across differences:

■ First, it focuses on designing service-learning experiences that are developmentally appropriate for elementary-age children, younger adolescents, and older adolescents.

■ Next, the chapter focuses on the potential for service-learning for two groups of youth who often get overlooked: youth with disabilities and marginalized youth (those who may be at risk, vulnerable, or disadvantaged and tend not to be involved in community organizations and activities). While these groups are often seen as recipients of service, they are also untapped resources for the community, and there is great potential in integrating them into service-learning efforts.

■ Finally, it looks at service-learning that engages families and intergenerational groups, emphasizing the potential of these kinds of experiences for asset building.

Elementary-Age Children (Ages 6 to 9)

Childhood is an important time for building a foundation of service and caring. "When volunteering becomes a natural part of a child's life at an early age, it adds an important dimension to the process of growing up and, ultimately shapes the adult that child becomes," write Susan J. Ellis, Anne Weisbord, and Katherine H. Noyes in *Children as Volunteers*.[5]

The elementary years are an active time when children's coordination improves and their energy overflows. Their world expands rapidly when they enter school, and they focus a lot of effort on building social skills and relationships. Elementary children learn through active participation, and they are developing the ability to complete tasks from start to finish. They can have short attention spans and be easily distracted. One reason may be that they are so curious and interested in everything!

Effective service-learning efforts for elementary-age children recognize the wide range of abilities and interests within this age group. Activities can

help to solidify children's emerging sense of care and compassion, giving them skills and opportunities to act on these values while also helping them learn to tackle big projects.

It's also important to remember that young children are concrete thinkers. They are much more likely to get interested and involved if the service and the recipient are tangible to them. This concreteness also makes service-learning a valuable tool for working with children. In *Teaching Young Children Through Service,* kindergarten teacher Ann Shoemaker writes: "Service-learning allows children to participate in 'hands-on' active learning; exactly what four to eight year olds need! The service element of service-learning helps children see an early connection between their learning and the world around them."[6]

Children benefit from service-learning efforts that:

■ Give them opportunities to select the activities;

■ Show immediate, tangible results, even on a small scale;

■ Are broken into smaller tasks and steps;

■ Challenge them without setting them up for failure;

■ Give them opportunities to interact with adults and older youth;

■ Offer options for participating based on their interests, abilities, and attention spans;

■ Allow for both individual and group involvement; and

■ Provide structure, direction, and focus for participation.

Younger Adolescents (Ages 10 to 15)

This period of life generally marks a change from the family-centered focus of childhood to an expanding sense of self and personal identity. However, while they are beginning to broaden their understanding of the world, 10- to 15-year-olds still tend to focus their energy on their immediate surroundings, interactions with their peers, and significant adults in their families, schools, neighborhoods, youth groups, congregations, and other parts of their "community." Because their world is defined primarily by their immediate close relationships, younger adolescents are better able to relate to the "here and now" than to abstract issues or ideas.

Younger adolescents also are typically pushing and testing boundaries, wanting to try each and every idea that comes along. Change for the sake of change is exciting, and repetitive activities may bore them quickly. Perhaps because they tend to see the possibilities as endless, these young people need and will appreciate structure and clear boundaries. Finally, younger adolescents have a great need for physical activity.

Effective service-learning efforts for younger adolescents can help them discover new interests and talents they didn't know they had. Programs for this age can also expose them to your organization's and community's social values. Ten- to 15-year-olds will also benefit from:

■ Opportunities to interact with other adults and youth;

■ Varied, one-time or short-term group experiences;

■ Focusing on *local, visible* needs;

■ Direct service experiences that offer immediate, tangible results;

■ Experiential, hands-on activities; and

■ Selecting service-learning issues and activities from a list of possible options.

Older Adolescents (Ages 16 to 18)

By the time they reach high school age, young people are usually more aware of and in tune with the world beyond them and with their own future. As their perspective expands, so does their ability to understand and address broader social issues. They have enough contact with institutions to understand how they affect people's lives. They also can empathize with people they haven't met. They appreciate the need

to look for longer-term solutions instead of immediate answers.

Older adolescents are trying to make sense of the big picture, to understand who they are and where they fit in the world. They seek strong interpersonal relationships. Although still interested in role experimentation and exploration, they have a clearer sense of their personal talents and gifts. Given opportunities, they can and will use these to address larger social issues and play meaningful roles in the community.

? QUESTIONS TO CONSIDER

▶ How does the information here about elementary–age children and younger and older adolescents reflect your experiences? How is your experience similar to or different from what's described?

▶ What has been the greatest lesson you have learned about working with one or more of these age groups?

▶ How are the young people you work with different from or similar to the general developmental patterns presented for these three age groups?

Although older adolescents have greater physical, cognitive, and social capacity for serving others, Search Institute research shows that they actually serve less than younger adolescents do.[7] One reason may be that they need more profound roles in planning and decision making. As their time becomes increasingly scarce, young people will begin to drop out of programs and activities unless they are given more responsibility and opportunities for leadership.

When done effectively, service-learning programs for older adolescents:

■ Offer variety and encourage serial or extended commitment to a single task or site;

■ Are geared to small-group and/or individual participation;

■ Provide an intentional mix of local, regional, and global opportunities for action and learning;

■ Link opportunities to provide direct service and immediate, tangible relief with needs for less tangible, longer-term change;

■ Actively involve participants in selecting appropriate issues and activities; and

■ Provide regular opportunities for program evaluation and reflection with peers and respected adults.

Young People with Disabilities

Engaging young people with disabilities in service-learning is an important opportunity, according to the Maryland Student Service Alliance:

> Students with disabilities are recipients of many special education and related services. Consequently, they are perceived as persons in need of assistance and are seldom seen as capable of giving assistance and making positive changes in the community. . . . Getting them involved in service-learning is one way to turn the tables—to empower them to have an active role in the school and community, and to give them the experience of being the helper rather than always the helpee.[8]

The Maryland Student Service Alliance offers a number of suggestions for effectively engaging young people with disabilities in service-learning. They include:

■ Identifying and designing service-learning projects to build on young people's strengths. Thus, for example, to include students with learning disabilities, you might focus reflection activities on discussion, not on writing;

■ Emphasizing basic life skills, such as communicating, writing, learning about work, caring for others, and preparing items for others;

■ Considering partial participation in which each young person takes a specific part of the project that matches her or his strengths. In this way, no student has to do everything, yet all are needed to complete the project;

■ Having each young person focus on and master a particular part of a project, then challenging her or him to try other roles and tasks as well;

■ Considering pairing young people with disabilities with young people who do not have disabilities in settings where each person's skills complement the other's;

■ Finding ways to adapt projects so that they more fully involve young people with various disabilities. Adaptations may include modifying equipment or materials, modifying or simplifying rules for participation, breaking activities down into smaller steps and discrete skills, or simplifying the overall activity;

■ Involving parents as much as possible in decision making, especially if they seem particularly overprotective or skeptical; and

■ Doing extra preparation with some young people, including having discussions about or role-playing appropriate behavior in the service setting.[9]

Table 3 shows sample projects and tips for success for students with a variety of disabilities.

? QUESTIONS TO CONSIDER

▶ What possibilities do you see for integrating young people with disabilities into your service-learning efforts?

▶ What experiences have you had in integrating youth with disabilities into your programming? If you haven't had much experience, who in your community could be a resource to assist you in being intentional in integrating these young people?

TABLE 3

SERVICE-LEARNING PROJECT POSSIBILITIES FOR STUDENTS WITH DISABILITIES

Disability	Sample Projects	Tips
Mental retardation	▶ Beautify school ▶ Serve at soup kitchen ▶ Sort items at food bank ▶ Visit nursing home	▶ Check accessibility ▶ Plan for short blocks of time ▶ Design hands-on activities
Learning disability	▶ Peer mediate ▶ Be reading buddies ▶ Tutor peers	▶ Give directions in multiple formats ▶ Place less emphasis on written work ▶ Design hands-on activities ▶ Delineate tasks clearly ▶ Structure activities well
Severe emotional disability	▶ Serve at soup kitchen ▶ Assemble MADD ribbons ▶ Tutor peers	▶ Structure activities well ▶ Use small groups ▶ Allow for lots of student decision making ▶ Develop individualized projects ▶ Use service as a reward
Physical disability	▶ Assemble items ▶ Package ▶ Entertain ▶ Other projects in accessible locations	▶ Ensure accessiblity, including workspace and lavatories ▶ Adapt equipment ▶ Bring project to kids ▶ Consider partial participation
Attention deficit with hyperactivity	▶ Tutor ▶ Organize notebooks ▶ Develop skills ▶ Review skills	▶ Design short, well-structured projects ▶ Pair with other students—peer buddies ▶ Have breaks with alternate activity planned ▶ Change tasks frequently ▶ Review ahead of time
Blind	▶ Assemble ▶ Create books on tape ▶ Entertain	▶ Pair with a buddy ▶ Watch for obstructions ▶ Determine whether Braille materials and Brailler are needed
Deaf	▶ Tutor peers ▶ Entertain ▶ Deaf awareness or advocacy	▶ Pair with a buddy ▶ Develop safety provisions and emergency signals at site ▶ Pair key signs with directions

Adapted with permission from Maryland Student Service Alliance, *Special Education Service-Learning Guide*, rev. ed. (Baltimore: Maryland Department of Education, 1993), 25.

Marginalized Young People

Service-learning has tremendous potential in the lives of marginalized youth—those who typically do not participate in community activities (sometimes described as vulnerable, disadvantaged, or at-risk youth). These young people—who often feel alienated from community institutions—rarely have opportunities to become resources to their communities, which typically view them as problems or with fear. Indeed, U.S. Department of Education research on high school seniors finds that low-income youth are much less likely to report performing community service than those with higher income levels.[10]

"Typically, disadvantaged youths are thought of as recipients of service, not givers," a Children's Defense Fund concludes. "But [service] efforts can play an instrumental role in reducing the chances of dropping out of school or other poor outcomes among participants. Given the proper guidance, direction, and supervision, young people respond well to the responsibility of service and sense the value of their efforts."[11]

Service-learning has the potential to strengthen many skills that marginalized youth need for future employment, skills that these young people may not see modeled in their families or neighborhoods. These include punctuality and reliability, responsibility for task completion, and getting along with others.[12] In addition, the hands-on approach to learning can be ideal for students who otherwise do not do well in—or feel connected to—school.

Furthermore, a Search Institute evaluation of the National Service-Learning Initiative and the Generator Schools Project concluded that students who are most disengaged from school when they entered a service-learning program were most likely to experience positive change. Students who were most at risk or more disengaged from school when they got involved in service-learning saw a number of positive changes during the time of their involvement. By the end, they were more likely to:

- Believe they were contributing to the community;
- Be less bored than in traditional classrooms;
- Be engaged in academic tasks and general learning; and
- Be more accepting of diversity.[13]

Maryanne Wonderlin, a school-based service-learning coordinator in Louisville, Kentucky, finds that kids who have a hard time sitting, carrying through with regular assignments, or being academically prepared are often most successful in service-learning. "Often, they are the ones that are most capable, since they're most likely to have had challenges at home that have forced them to be more streetwise than others. Service learning gives these kids a chance to be leaders."

Young people who have been marginalized may need extra encouragement to get involved. Furthermore, it may take longer to build trust and for them to respond well to being treated respectfully and as a resource, not as a problem. However, in many cases, the extra effort is worth it in terms of the creativity and leadership that these young people can bring—skills and abilities they may have been using in destructive ways. Novella Zett Keith writes that some behaviors that are considered deviant can actually be gifts:

> *Assertive cultural, art and music forms such as rap, breakdancing, graffiti murals and the like, speak of a creativity that persists in the midst of want. . . . These activities are not just individual, but are supported by peer groups, which call forth extraordinary commitment. This is not to romanticize such involvements, the darker side of which is gang membership; it is merely to call attention not only, as is common, to their deviance, but also to their capacities.[14]*

One of the dangers in specifically targeting marginalized youth is that people will design service-learning programs specifically for these young people. Such an approach may only exacerbate the tendency to separate one group of young people from others. Indeed, service-learning projects can be opportunities for all young people to participate on an equal footing and build relationships across differences, with all contributing according to their strengths.[15]

The keys to effectively engaging marginalized young people in service-learning are essentially the same as for any other group of youth. However, because of their past experiences and the potential for mistrust, it can be helpful to emphasize the following elements:

■ Creating a group environment in which young people feel safe, well connected, and like they belong;

■ Inviting them to identify the issues and concerns that they want to address;

■ Setting clear boundaries and expectations for behavior;

■ Challenging them to use their gifts, talents, and energy to do benefit others;

■ Increasing their responsibilities as they have early successes; and

■ Inviting responsible adults to serve as mentors, role models, and guides.

Families

Families play a critical role in young people being interested in serving others. Yet rarely do service-learning programs tap the potential impact and opportunity of designing experiences that intentionally encourage families to serve together. Actively engaging families in service-learning experiences can benefit all types of youth-serving organizations:

■ It offers schools a powerful approach to parental involvement (asset #6) in which parents are role models and partners with their children in providing service to others.

■ It offers youth organizations a concrete opportunity to connect with and support families in the community.

■ It offers congregations an exceptional vehicle for helping parents nurture faith in their children and pass along their values and priorities.[16]

QUESTIONS TO CONSIDER

▶ When have you seen engagement in service-learning bring out previously unrecognized gifts and talents in marginalized young people?

▶ What concerns can you anticipate others will have about seeking to involve marginalized youth in your service-learning efforts? How can you address those concerns?

▶ Who in your organization can be resources for helping engage marginalized young people most effectively?

In all cases, service-learning offers families an opportunity to spend time together doing meaningful work, and a context for talking about the family's values, priorities, beliefs, and worldview. "Family volunteering helps develop . . . stronger bonds by allowing family members to see each other in new roles and gain new appreciation for each other," says Virginia T. Austin of the Points of Light Foundation. "Adults are no longer automatic leaders. Volunteering as a family gives young people the opportunity to lead and direct."[17]

Designing service-learning experiences with families in mind is a high priority for St. John of the Cross Catholic Church in Middlebury, Connecticut, according to Tom Bright, who serves as the parish's justice coordinator and is also the service and justice coordinator for the Center for Ministry Development in Naugatuck, Connecticut. The parish found that families really wanted to be involved, but they didn't know how and were uncomfortable engaging in service by themselves without guidance.

So the parish identified a variety of service opportunities and hosted a service fair in which families heard about different possibilities for involvement. Then families were asked to commit to one of the options. Later someone followed up with them. The parish's goal was to move families toward greater and greater involvement and commitment.

? QUESTIONS TO CONSIDER

▶ In what ways does your organization connect to families? How might you build on these connections to engage them in service-learning?

▶ What kinds of issues concern families in your community? How might those concerns become entry points for service-learning?

▶ Where are families already engaged in service in your community or organization? How can you build on that involvement by connecting other families—or helping those already involved to be more intentional about reflection and learning?

One year, families were invited to help refresh the facilities of a homeless shelter in a nearby community. For a day, families painted and cleaned. In the process, they were exposed to the need, became comfortable with the location, and had the satisfaction of immediate results.

The next year, the congregation organized people who had experience serving in the shelter who were willing to be mentors for interested families. The mentors visited with the families to prepare them for their experience, and then served alongside them on their first evening at the shelter. Afterward, they reflected together about the experience. Before long,

many of the families were comfortable and committed to serving in the shelter on a monthly basis.

Designing service-learning for families raises additional challenges. These include issues of scheduling as well as concerns that teenagers sometimes do not want their parents around. Here are some issues to consider in developing service-learning opportunities for families:

■ Focus on activities to which people of all ages—from young children through adulthood—can contribute meaningfully.

■ Emphasize the learning and modeling opportunity to parents. A survey of families by the Family Matters program of the Points of Light Foundation found that the top reason agency leaders say families volunteer together is "to teach values of service and community involvement" to their children (70 percent).[18]

■ Prepare families well. Provide background information that can address any misperceptions, and train families in site-specific skills.

■ Be creative and flexible with scheduling. Be clear about expectations and time commitments.

■ Offer a variety of options and opportunities for families to get involved, depending on their schedule, interests, and level of commitment. Identify some opportunities that individual families can do on their own as well as opportunities for several families to serve together.

■ Offer families guidance and opportunities for doing service projects on their own time and schedule. Develop printed resources to give them to use for reflection at home.

■ Challenge all family members to work side by side in meaningful roles, rather than falling into patterns whereby parents provide the leadership and have primary responsibilities.

■ Even if families are not actively involved in the service-learning project, keep them informed about what's happening. Encourage them to talk with their children about what they are experiencing and learning.

Intergenerational Groups

One of the major themes in asset building is nurturing relationships across generations. The benefits and potential of linking generations through service-learning are captured in a report from the Center on Rural Elderly at the University of Missouri. Some of these include:

■ Increased understanding between and among generations. "Youth have an opportunity to see what it's like to be old. Older people gain insights into the lives, value systems, and problems of youth";

■ Opportunities for new relationships at a time when seniors may be losing friends and relatives and when young people often have grandparents who live far away; and

■ Opportunities for the community to mobilize untapped volunteer resources in both generations who may be inactive or ignored.[19]

Traditionally, service-learning has built intergenerational relationships primarily in two ways:

■ Having young people engage in service with and for senior citizens. These projects might include "adopt-a-grandparent" or collecting oral histories; and

■ Recognizing the important role that adult sponsors and allies play in service-learning experiences and emphasizing the need for adequate adult involvement and supervision in service-learning efforts.

Both of these approaches are important strategies for building intergenerational relationships through service-learning. In addition, organizations and communities are recognizing the potential of people of all ages—from young to middle-aged to elderly—serving others together. And while such an approach may be difficult to undertake in settings that primarily serve one age group (such as schools), the potential is great in organizations that engage people of all ages, including community initiatives, community agencies, volunteer centers, and congregations.

How do you design effective service-learning programs for intergenerational groups? Once again, the basic principles of service-learning also apply to intergenerational service-learning. In addition, consider the following suggestions:

■ Involve all generations in planning and preparation;

■ Make sure the experience is meaningful and beneficial to all generations. Ensure that all ages can give as well as receive;

■ Encourage cross-generation conversation, sharing, and relationship building. This can be enhanced by helping people in each generation understand the other generations more fully so that they don't begin their time together with numerous misperceptions and stereotypes;

■ Recognize both the strengths and limitations of the people involved. For example, elderly participants have a great deal of wisdom, experience, and perspective. Many also find that their bodies are slowing down, and their hearing and eyesight are diminished; and

■ Be explicit and intentional in nurturing mutual respect and understanding across generations. This can be accomplished, for example, by ensuring that people from all generations have active leadership roles in planning and executing projects. It also can be addressed by ensuring that no single generation dominates times of reflection.

Developing intergenerational programs doesn't have to begin from scratch. Often, existing service-learning activities can be broadened to include other generations. If, for example, you already have a strong youth service-learning program, look for ways to incorporate other ages into those experiences to make them more intergenerational. Or identify specific components of existing programs that would naturally work as intergenerational experiences.

Intergenerational service-learning has particular power for community-wide asset-building initiatives, since it can be an exceptional opportunity to

? QUESTIONS TO CONSIDER

▶ When have you seen groups of young people and adults working together? What made those experiences successful? What issues had to be addressed?

▶ What kinds of activities does your organization already engage in that include people from several generations? How might those activities be springboards for intergenerational service-learning?

build community and relationships across all age groups. Multiple organizations in the community—schools, congregations, service clubs, community agencies, neighborhood associations, and senior citizen centers—can all be involved actively in planning events and engaging their constituencies in serving others and the community. Figure 10 offers a few ideas for short-term projects that could be done on a community-wide basis.

Young people can often be the catalysts for involvement by other ages. As young people have positive service-learning experiences on their own, others see their enthusiasm and can be eager to join in if invited. In these cases, the young people become the teachers and mentors to others who get involved.

Assessing the Servers' Readiness

This chapter has presented general guidelines for engaging different groups in service-learning. In addition to these general guidelines, it is important to look at your specific group's current realities so that you can design experiences that meet their needs and help to ensure that the effort will be successful. Here are some questions to ask about your group:

■ What kind of experience in serving others do the young people, families, or intergenerational groups you seek to engage have? Do they already have experience in service-learning (perhaps in another setting)? Have they been involved in ongoing volunteer work? Have they only done informal service? What kinds of experiences stretch them to grow without pushing them so far that they become discouraged or disappointed?

■ Does your group or class already have strong relationships? Or do you need to identify initial projects that will emphasize relationship building?

■ What resources are available among the servers that could be tapped in your service-learning effort? What skills and experiences do they bring? What opportunities might they have access to that would be valuable to your service-learning goals?

The answers to these kinds of questions help you identify a "next step" service-learning option that challenges people to grow without setting them up for frustration or failure. They also set the stage for other elements of planning an experience that will help people grow through service-learning.

Sorting Out the Possibilities

This chapter has identified seven different groups to engage in service-learning. How do you decide how to focus your efforts? Worksheet 4 will help you sort out the possibilities. In addition, consider these suggestions:

■ Build on current strengths, connections, and capacities. If you're a middle school teacher, you may want to focus your energy on the young people in that classroom. But, because of the diversity of youth, you may also want to examine whether young people with disabilities and marginalized youth could be more fully integrated.

■ Don't try to design a unique program for each group. Such an approach could only exacerbate differences and divisions. Rather, use the information on different groups to shape how you design activities that may involve several groups.

FIGURE 10

IDEAS FOR COMMUNITY-WIDE SERVICE PROJECTS

Community-wide service projects have lots of asset-building potential. Not only can they bring together people of all different ages who share a commitment to the community, they can draw attention to your asset-building efforts. Here are some ideas for short-term projects to try:

▶ Have seasonal service projects. In the fall, have residents replace and clean gutters, rake and bag leaves, and winterize homes of those in need. In the spring, have community-wide raking, weeding, and planting.

▶ Hold a community-wide blood drive.

▶ Organize a day when people donate their expertise, such as having barbers giving free haircuts, mechanics providing free oil changes, dentists giving free dental exams, police officers installing deadbolts on doors, and nurses giving hearing and eye exams.

▶ Be creative in the items that you collect for donations. For example, collect wigs for cancer patients, teddy bears and other stuffed animals for a pediatric ward, and underwear and socks for homeless people.

▶ Start babies out right. Collect diapers, baby food, baby clothes, infant car seats, and the many things that young children need for their health and safety. Or have a baby-food drive to stock the shelves of food banks.

▶ Paint cheery murals over graffiti or crumbling walls in the community.

▶ Build a community playground or transform an unused room or building into a community drop-in center.

▶ Have a community-wide yard sale where all the proceeds go to a local service organization.

▶ Collect used appliances that still work to donate to individuals of service organizations who need them.

▶ Have a loose-change drive or a penny drive. Call it "Pennies from _____ (your community name)." Collect coins for a month and donate the money to a local cause.

▶ Have a bicycle and tricycle repair day at a central location in the community.

WHICH GROUPS WILL YOU INCLUDE
IN SERVICE-LEARNING?

Use this worksheet with your leadership team to explore options for engaging different groups more intentionally in service-learning. In the "Current Realities" column, identify current involvement, connections, and challenges. In the "Possibilities to Explore" column, brainstorm ways your effort might include each group more effectively. Then select those possibilities you want to pursue.

Group	Current Realities	Possibilities to Explore
Elementary-age children		
Younger adolescent		
Older adolescents		
Youth with disabilities		
Marginalized youth		
Families		
Intergenerational groups		

■ Recognize the need for options. Every person does not have to participate in every project. The goal over time is to provide options that allow all to participate in ways that fit their priorities, readiness, and interests.

One of the dangers in highlighting the unique issues for various groups in service-learning is that it can leave the impression that you have to do service-learning in radically different ways for different groups. While it is important to be aware of and sensitive to each group's specific needs, issues, and opportunities, it is even more important to strengthen the core elements of service-learning: careful planning, meaningful action, guided reflection, and recognition. These foundational components provide the basic architecture; the differences needed to shape involvement for different groups are the final touches to ensure that all young people have the opportunity to serve and learn.

CHAPTER 4

SETTING THE STAGE
FOR SERVICE-LEARNING

You're ready. You know service-learning can make a difference for kids. You're committed to asset building. You know that kids could really do a lot to address important community issues. Your organization is committed, and you know what young people and intergenerational groups you want to involve. Time to start planning service projects, right?

Not quite.

You could plan a single service project. But your efforts will have a more lasting impact if you take the time to set the stage for service-learning in ways that will guide and support ongoing efforts to engage youth in service-learning. This preplanning is important for several reasons:

- Service-learning has its greatest impact when young people are engaged over significant periods of time. While some individual projects may offer that kind of sustained involvement, you're more likely to achieve it through "serial participation"—engaging young people in a series of service-learning experiences that are tied together with shared themes, goals, and learning.

- It is more efficient to lay a broad foundation. Once you have some basic elements in place (such as learning objectives and safety guidelines), they can be available for multiple projects.

- Your organization can offer or broker multiple options for involvement based on different interests, sched-

ules, and preferences—all tie together, since they are grounded upon the same foundation.

- You provide the infrastructure and organizational support and boundaries needed for young people to be successful as they plan and lead specific service-learning activities.

Chapters 2 and 3 focused on two critical tasks in setting the stage: building support and leadership, and designing efforts based on the specific young people (or intergenerational groups) who will be involved. This chapter identifies six additional tasks:

- Setting overall goals for your efforts;
- Identifying available resources and opportunities;
- Building relationships with volunteer organizations and agencies;
- Developing a base of funding;
- Managing risk and ensuring safety; and
- Cultivating a culture of service.

Keep in mind that these tasks are interlocking, not sequential. So while this guide organizes them in a particular order, you'll likely discover that you're doing pieces of all of these simultaneously, and one will influence and shape the others. As you get further along in the process, you may find that you need to revisit earlier tasks. So don't feel tied to the order or categories of information offered in this chapter. Rather, use the ideas in ways that fit your organization.

Establishing Overall Goals for Your Efforts

A vision suggests the possibilities for an asset-based service-learning emphasis. For your program to have the kind of impact you hope for, it's just as important to identify specific goals before you begin planning specific activities with youth, since these goals will help focus and shape your planning. By setting these goals in advance, young people can plan a variety of service projects that all tie together around these core goals.

There are at least three goal areas for your leadership group to consider: asset-building or development goals, learning goals, and service goals. Use Worksheet 5 to record your organization's overall goals in each of these three areas.

In developing these goals, it is important to think of them as reinforcing each other. Barry Fenstermacher writes: "[T]he goal is to blend service and learning goals and activities in such a way that the two reinforce each other and produce a greater impact than either could produce alone."[1] Though Fenstermacher focuses on learning and service goals, his point extends to all three goals.

Growth and development goals—Many of your growth and development goals can tie directly to asset building. Engagement in service is, by itself, an asset, and virtually any quality service-learning experience builds some of the assets, even if it's not intentional. However, setting goals related to asset building has three benefits:

1. It can reinforce elements of effective service-learning. For example, a focus on asset #32 (planning and decision making) emphasizes the importance of young people being involved in leading the service-learning effort.

2. It can give a well-rounded perspective on the impact of service-learning on young people. For example, asset #3 (other adult relationships) emphasizes the importance of the relationships with adult

sponsors and allies, and the value of service projects that connect young people to other generations.

3. It can suggest activities and forms of service that might not otherwise have been identified. Asset #36 (peaceful conflict resolution) triggers a wide variety of service-learning possibilities. So does asset #17 (creative activities), but the types of service possibilities are totally different.

Focusing goals on one category of assets or a few individual assets does not mean those are the only assets the service-learning experience will intentionally build. Rather, it simply provides a starting point for emphasis. Later chapters show ways in which the assets and asset categories can be filters and guides for shaping all service-learning experiences.

In addition to the general development goals related to asset building, you'll want to think about development goals related to the specific characteristics and life experiences of the young people and the dynamics within the group. Answering two questions could identify additional growth and development goals:

■ What skills do you want young people to build or strengthen?

■ How well do the young people already know each other? What goals do you have to build their relationships and trust?

One particular area of growth for many students comes through relationships with community members that form during service-learning projects. As Janet Eyler and Dwight Giles Jr. write, "For many students, a brief service project may be the first time they are confronted with people whose life experiences are very different from their own, and such an experience may be very emotionally powerful."[2]

Learning goals—An emphasis on learning is what differentiates service-learning from other forms of service and volunteering. *The Standards of Quality for School-Based Service-Learning* published by the Alliance for Service-Learning in Education Reform

YOUR OVERALL GOALS FOR SERVICE-LEARNING

This worksheet offers an opportunity to record your overall service-learning goals for the next year. Once set, these goals can help your organization select and design projects.

1. What are your major growth and development goals? In what areas do you want young people to have a stronger base of developmental assets? How do you want the group to grow?

_____

_____

_____

_____

_____

_____

_____

_____

_____

2. What are your major learning goals?

_____

_____

_____

_____

_____

_____

_____

_____

_____

3. What are your major service goals? What kind of impact do you want to have?

_____

_____

_____

_____

_____

_____

_____

_____

_____

put it this way: "Service-learning efforts should begin with clearly articulated learning goals, to be achieved through structured preparation and reflection—discussion, writing, reading, observation—and the service itself."[3] Educational theorist John Dewey suggested that, to be truly educative, projects must:

■ Generate interest;

■ Be intrinsically worthwhile;

■ Present problems that awaken curiosity and a demand for learning; and

■ Cover enough time to foster development.[4]

The specific learning goals will vary widely based on the age of young people involved, the organization's learning focus, and the specific content areas. In a school, for example, the learning goals for a project with a homeless shelter may tie to a specific subject area, such as social studies. A congregational youth group might engage in the same activity, but the goal might be to deepen their understanding of their faith tradition's mandate to care for the poor. Table 4 presents the variety of learning goals that can be possible for a particular project.

In setting learning goals, it can be helpful to think of the variety of options available for connecting service-learning to your organization's learning goals. Here are some of the variables to consider:

■ Will the service-learning experience be integral to the learning curriculum or will it be cocurricular? For example, some schools focus their service-learning efforts through after-school clubs and organizations. Others make it a core part of the curriculum. Some congregations make service-learning an integral part of religious education (such as confirmation, Bar/Bat Mitzvah). Others plan separate service projects and options.

■ How formally will students be evaluated or graded on their learning through service? Will they receive credit (e.g., academic credit, merit badges.) for their service involvement?

■ Will the learning focus on one subject area, or will it be interdisciplinary?

■ Are your learning goals more academic, vocational, or societal? Do you want young people to learn and apply academic learning (math, science, political science, etc.)? Or are you more interested in their building specific vocational skills? Or do you want them to learn about different cultures and life experiences?

■ Will the learning be formal and structured, or will it be informal?

Each of these variables will affect how you shape your service-learning efforts. For example, the more formal you make the learning goals, the more you will have to emphasize reflection, interpretation, and application. It will also determine the kinds of projects you take on to ensure that young people have specific opportunities to learn through practice.

Service goals—The third type of goal relates to the service performed or the impact in the community. These goals should be developed jointly with the young people who will serve and the community being served. These goals will change for each service-learning project and are addressed in Chapter 5 on preparing for a service-learning experience.

However, one area of service goals needs to be addressed early: where will you serve? There are three general settings to consider: within your organization, within your community, and beyond your community. Table 5 offers some examples, strengths, and limitations of service-learning in each setting.

The context addresses the issue of how broad your service impact will be. For many, the motto "Think Globally, Act Locally" captures an essential spirit of service-learning: one group can't take on all the world's problems at one time, but local efforts are an important step in learning about and dealing with state, national, and even global problems.

For example, young people can learn about hunger by working at a food bank. Those local experiences can provide insight into the problem of

TABLE 4

SAMPLE LEARNING EMPHASES IN DIFFERENT SETTINGS

Project	School	Youth Organization	Congregation
Organizing a food drive for a food shelf	▶ Home economics: nutrition and food costs	▶ Job skills such as keeping inventory ▶ Leadership skills in planning the drive	▶ The responsibility of people of faith to care for the poor
Tutoring younger children	▶ English: improving reading and writing skills ▶ Social studies: understanding child development	▶ Educational enrichment ▶ Social skills (talking with younger children, problem solving, etc.)	▶ Developing spiritual qualities such as patience and caring
Studying and cleaning up a river or lake	▶ Science: understanding ecological systems	▶ Appreciating nature ▶ Responsibility for the environment	▶ A faith perspective on the environment and creation
Building a home for a low-income family	▶ Industrial arts: carpentry, masonry, project planning, and other skills	▶ Planning and organizing skills ▶ Understanding different people	▶ Social and economic justice from a faith perspective
Participating in a voter registration drive	▶ Civics: understanding the political process	▶ Civic responsibility ▶ Commitment to the community	▶ The responsibility of people of faith to participate in the political process
Developing a presentation about racism	▶ History: learning about slavery and the civil rights movement	▶ Appreciating differences in society	▶ Faith perspectives on racial justice and reconciliation

TABLE 5

WHERE WILL YOU OFFER SERVICE?

This chart offers examples, strengths, and limitations of different contexts in which young people, families, and intergenerational groups may do service-learning projects. Many organizations find it valuable to engage in service in different contexts over time.

Setting	Examples	Possible Strengths	Possible Limitations
Within the organization	▶ Improving facilities (painting, cleanup, artwork) ▶ Assisting others within the organization (younger children, senior citizens) ▶ Leading or planning activities and programs	▶ Easy place to start because of the low risk involved ▶ Often easiest to do ▶ No transportation needed ▶ Meets organizational needs ▶ Gives young people visibility within the organization	▶ Does not draw young people to build the habit of caring for others in the community and world ▶ Limits options for deepening understanding across differences ▶ May not be interesting or motivating to youth
Within the community	▶ Working with a local agency to provide services to children, families, or senior citizens, or meet other community needs ▶ Offering programming for children in the community ▶ Doing ecological studies or cleanup	▶ Can engage in service over an extended period of time ▶ Highlights young people as resources to their community ▶ Can be done in relatively short segments of time ▶ Easy for families and intergenerational groups to participate ▶ Can expose young people to national and global issues ▶ Sites are relatively easy to reach ▶ Others in the organization and community can be involved ▶ Helps young people identify with their own neighborhood ▶ Can build a commitment to the local community	▶ Requires transportation ▶ May not be interesting or motivating to youth ▶ Schedule conflicts can be significant if the service is spread out over time
Beyond the community	▶ Taking weeklong work trips to economically distressed areas of the country ▶ Building a hospital or digging wells in a developing country ▶ Providing music, education, or other programs for children in another community during the summer ▶ Doing ecological restoration in a wilderness area	▶ Highlights connections between their own community and larger social issues ▶ Exposes young people to other places, cultures, and issues ▶ Provides a memorable retreat-like experience of bonding and growth ▶ Can generate lots of interest and energy among youth and in the organization ▶ Models effective organizational and service principles	▶ Can be costly and time-consuming to plan and carry out ▶ Provides less opportunity for young people to build long-term relationships in the community ▶ Can reinforce a false notion that you have to leave home to serve

hunger nationally. So you don't have to travel far or introduce young people to new and startling environments in order to get the most out of service-learning.

When it is effective, service-learning offers young people much more than an experience. It also introduces them to a *process,* a way of learning about and taking action on a wide variety of issues and concerns. As their comfort level grows and other opportunities arise, so will their willingness to explore new sites, issues, and activities. You can encourage this by stressing the idea that service is not an "either-or" activity (*either* our needs *or* the needs of others; *either* local *or* global), but rather it is "both-and" (*both* within *and* beyond the organization; local *and* state *and* national *and* global).

? QUESTIONS TO CONSIDER

▶ Do you have specific learning goals tied to your service-learning efforts? What are they?

▶ Which assets do you hope to nurture in young people through your service-learning efforts?

▶ How do your service-learning goals fit with other goals in your organization?

▶ Does your organization already have goals for service and/or service-learning? Are they consistent with your goals for your program? If not, why not?

▶ What time frame are you thinking of for your short-term goals? Six months? Nine months? One year?

As you build a comprehensive service-learning program, you'll likely want to provide a mixture of opportunities in several of these settings. Not only will different types of experiences attract different people to service-learning, it will also offer variety and reinforce the importance of serving others in all areas of our lives.

Keep in mind, too, that you can address national

and international issues through indirect service without ever physically leaving your building. Often these kinds of indirect experiences of providing resources, supplies, and other material goods to meet needs elsewhere can be entry points for service-learning. They can also be an important part of preparation and follow-up for an off-site experience.

Identifying Available Resources and Opportunities

Often when people begin planning service-learning experiences, they start by identifying needs. But while it is important to address real needs through the service provided, it is just as important to select projects based on the available resources. Once you know what resources are available, you'll be able to identify projects that your class or group truly can accomplish. Consider three types of resources:

People resources—As Chapter 3 emphasized, it is important to select projects that match the group who will be providing the service, whether it's a group of young people, families, or an intergenerational group. The group's size, skills, service experience, and maturity all play a role in shaping your project. If, for example, you have an intergenerational group in which the skills and experience vary widely, you'll need to identify projects that call for a wide variety of skills and experience.

Financial resources—Later in this chapter, we address various ways to identify funding to support your service-learning efforts. But before you even begin, you need to have a realistic sense of what level of funding is realistic. Historically, how much money has been available from your organization and other funders to support service-learning projects? How much, if anything, can young people and their families contribute to the effort? What other funding might be accessible?

Logistical resources—Service-learning projects can have many logistical details, from transportation to ordering materials to coordinating schedules to providing general office support. What kind of capacity does your organization have to provide this kind of support? In some cases you may find creative solutions; in other cases you may have to make changes or sacrifices. For example, if transportation is a problem, you'll probably have to choose a local site that young people can walk to.

As you examine available resources, keep in mind that some may not be readily apparent. Your organization may have a volunteer or benefactor who runs a bus service who would be willing to provide transportation. A local lumberyard, printer, or other community-minded business may be interested in supplying materials or services free or at cost. These kinds of contributions can give your group's service-learning efforts far greater potential for impact than you might otherwise have imagined.

Available opportunities—You don't have to start with something new. There may already be within your organization existing opportunities for service in which you could engage young people. Or there may be existing youth service projects that could be enhanced for learning by adding intentional preparation and reflection. Here are some places to look:

■ Projects that people in your organization already do;

■ Organizations where families already volunteer;

■ Places and issues to which young people are already connected through other organizations (for example, you may learn that several young people in a school class already volunteer at the zoo as part of an after-school program);

■ Community organizations and social service agencies that already have volunteer programs in place and have experience including young people in projects; and

■ Community service clubs (Rotary, Lions, Kiwanis, Junior League) and fraternal organizations (Elks, Lutheran Brotherhood, Knights of Columbus) that regularly organize service and volunteering events.

In short, build on what others are already doing, both within your organization and beyond. In a

school, another class, teacher, or group may have a lot of experience. In a congregation, a group of adults may already be involved. In a youth organization, there may be another department that emphasizes volunteering.

The possibilities are almost endless for connecting with people outside your organization as well.

QUESTIONS TO CONSIDER

▶ What kinds of skills, gifts, and abilities do the young people you work with have that they could offer to others through service-learning?

▶ What kinds of resources are most plentiful for your efforts? What kinds are most difficult to find?

▶ What other service-related efforts are already under way in your organization or community? How could you build upon these for service-learning?

For example, you could pair up with a nearby organization that runs a weeklong service camp or a clown group that visits children's wards in local hospitals. Your young people will benefit from working alongside other youth with more experience who share their enthusiasm for service.

You could also join established programs for young people or form partnerships with local youth workers to design a more ambitions program than you could offer on your own. If your group is organized on a state, regional, or national level, it may have resources committed to youth or justice and service that could be tapped for your program.

Within the wider civic community, national celebrations like Martin Luther King Jr. Day, Earth Day, National Youth Service Day, or World Food Day can easily become springboards for service. Local events may already be organized. If not, a service-learning project should be relatively easy to organize, given the large amounts of information that are usually available about these days.

Building Relationships with Volunteer Organizations and Agencies

If you are interested in working with an agency or organization that is unfamiliar with or uncomfortable with youth service, you'll help yourself, your young people, and your program if you do some relationship building up front. Many agencies historically have relied on adult volunteers and may be reluctant to work with young people. Sometimes they have stereotypes of youth and what they can and can't do.

A good way to begin forming a relationship is to schedule a meeting with the director, volunteer coordinator, or other key staff. If you have a few young people who have experience with service-learning and can articulate what they did and the impact it had, bring them with you. Listening to young people talk about the power of service-learning is often one of the best ways to convince skeptics of its value. Other ways to build relationships are to:

■ Encourage agency staff to visit other sites where youth are serving. Go with them and talk about the work young people are doing, the concerns they have about youth volunteers in their own organization, and questions they have about your program.

■ Show agency staff pictures of work that has been done by young people, letters or journal entries from young people or adults that reflect positive service-learning experiences, or other artifacts of successful youth service projects.

■ Start with short-term, low-risk projects that give adults in the organization opportunities to build relationships with the young people.[5]

If an agency or organization is still uncomfortable with the idea of youth service-learning, it's probably a good idea to find somewhere else to focus your energy. If the people working with and supervising them don't believe in young people's capabilities, the young people are unlikely to have a positive, rewarding experience.

Building relationships with agencies has great

? **QUESTIONS TO CONSIDER**

▶ What experience, if any, has your organization had in working with local agencies and community organizations? How can you build on those relationships and experiences?

▶ Where have you seen young people already providing volunteer service in the community? How might you approach those organizations as possible partners—or to help you identify the best ways to approach other agencies in the community?

rewards, though, according to Janet Shuster, a school-based service-learning coordinator in Kirkwood, Missouri. "Six years ago agencies were interested but not willing to take on volunteers under age 18," she says. But almost full employment has forced social service providers to look far and wide for motivated volunteers. In addition, training by such organizations as the United Way of America has reinforced the notion that young people can be important resources. "Even grade school children can be of service by drawing pictures for decorations," added Shuster.

She invites agency representatives to meet with youth during the preparation phase of a project. "Jobs as simple as stuffing envelopes need a context," she explained, adding that young people's physical presence on-site isn't always necessary to accomplish important service work.

Raising Funds to Support Your Efforts

Service-learning doesn't have to be expensive. In fact, a worthwhile project can be done with little or no money at all. However, if you need funding for a specific project or to support an ongoing service-learning program (including time for people to plan and coordinate), there are many possible sources of funding.

Your organization—Is money set aside for youth programs, experiential learning, field trips, or service projects? If not, think about how you might approach your organization's leadership to seek new funding, either out of discretionary funds or as part of the next fiscal year's budget—a clear sign of a commitment to service-learning.

It may also be that funding is available to support other activities that can be accomplished through service-learning. For example, your school may have money available for curriculum development. It could be applied to designing the reflection and learning elements of service-learning. In a congregation, there may be money available to support youth activities or trips. This funding could easily be applied to service-learning activities.

Another strategy for getting your organization to support service-learning financially is to seek out allies who may have access to funding. Look for ways to form mutually beneficial partnerships by including them on your leadership team, focusing on issues about which you share mutual concern, and engaging them in service along with your youth.

There may also be special funds or groups affiliated with your organization that would be interested in supporting youth service-learning. In schools, these may include parent-teacher organizations. In congregations, there may be an endowed fund or a benevolence budget that could be tapped. Identifying these possibilities can be effective ways to gain financial support, particularly if your organization isn't ready to make service-learning an ongoing budget item.

Partner organizations—If you're working with an agency in the community to provide service, they may have funding to cover some or all of the costs of your project. For example, agencies that can't afford to hire painters can often find money for paint, supplies, and snacks if the labor is provided free of charge.

Local service organizations or foundations—Most communities have service organizations (Rotary, Lions, Junior League, Chamber of Commerce, fraternal organizations, ethnic organizations) and local foundations that often offer small contributions or grants to support youth service projects. Not only do these sources offer the potential of funding, but young people can also learn the skill of writing and presenting a funding proposal.

Families and other allies—You may decide to ask families and other allies within your organization to support your service-learning efforts by contributing a small fee to support your program or particular projects. However, take precautions to ensure that families without adequate financial resources are not eliminated from participation.

Young people themselves—Many young people have significant discretionary income. Too often, we forget to invite them to contribute their money along with their time. Of course, there can be problems with asking them to give. These may include a concern about taking advantage of youth or making those without income feel particularly uncomfortable.

At the same time, asking young people to give begins to nurture the habit of philanthropic giving that can continue into adulthood. Furthermore, young people are more likely to give to a cause with which they are intimately involved than to an abstract need somewhere else in the world. So while there are certainly reasons to be cautious in asking young people to give, there are also important benefits to be considered.

Fund-raising—Fund-raising is often an inevitable part of service-learning projects. Unless you are careful, these activities can consume a tremendous amount of time and energy for relatively few dollars. At the same time, they can be fun, group-building activities.

If you decide to use fund-raisers to support all or part of your service-learning activities, consider these tips:

■ Select fund-raisers that are fun for youth and that people enjoy supporting.

■ Make sure that the amount of funds you can raise is worth the effort. This can be particularly problematic when a fund-raiser involves spending a significant amount on supplies and overhead. For example, a banquet can be a great fund-raiser, but it also can be costly to host. If too few people attend, you could use up most of the money raised just paying for the event.

■ Ask local businesses to donate supplies and prizes for the fund-raiser so that you won't have to pay for them.

■ Consider ways to tie fund-raising to the focus of your service-learning effort. For example, if you're raising money to travel to a developing country, consider selling crafts from that country. Or have young people put on a play or concert (with admission fees as the fund-raising) that educates people about the site or issue.

■ Partner with other groups in the organization or community who have experience in fund-raising. In schools, for example, the parent-teacher organization may have experience and ideas that would benefit your efforts. Service clubs in the community also may be interested in supporting your service-learning efforts.

■ Use the fund-raising campaign as another learning opportunity for young people. Have them plan, organize, and carry out the fund-raiser.

QUESTIONS TO CONSIDER

▶ What funds are already available for your use?

▶ Who can you talk to about meeting your remaining funding needs?

▶ What role do you want fund-raising to play?

▶ How much financial support are you comfortable asking for from families, your organization, or other sources?

▶ What kinds of information and skills might young people be able to learn while also meeting funding needs?

■ Avoid fund-raisers that put young people at risk. These may include going from door to door. (If you use this type of fund-raiser, follow the guidelines established by the National Center for Missing and Exploited Children: **1.** Don't go alone. **2.** Have an adult nearby. **3.** Sell only in your own community, preferably only to people you know.)[6]

Youth-run foundations—Usually when we think of fund-raising for service projects, we imagine bake sales, auctions, car washes, and similar efforts designed to get enough money together for a specific project. Recently, though, "minifoundations" have been developed as part of service-learning programs. In these efforts, young people learn about how philanthropic foundations operate by raising funds, assessing needs, requesting and evaluating proposals, and giving and monitoring grants.

One well-developed model of youth-run foundations is the Student Service and Philanthropy Project (SSPP), put together by the Surdna Foundation and the New York City Public Schools. It began in 1991 in three New York City high schools and has spread to more than 30 towns and cities across the United States.

SSPP is, in itself, a service-learning project. Students participate in extensive classwork to understand the history and role of foundations, appreciate community needs, set up a foundation, and develop leadership skills. At the same time, they are actively engaged in developing a student foundation that is designed to provide funding for students to meet community needs. Under the leadership of project director Linda M. Frank, the Surdna Foundation has begun encouraging other communities to learn from and adopt this model.[7]

The SSPP approach is one of the more fully developed models of a youth-run foundation. Many other communities and organizations establish youth committees to raise funds and then give grants to support youth-initiated service-learning projects. Start-up funding could be raised through traditional fund-raisers, or community foundations, businesses, and others can give the committee an annual grant that it can then disburse to support a variety of youth service-learning activities in the organization or community.

Managing Risk and Ensuring Safety

Taking young people out of their usual environment and introducing them to new tasks, skills, and people inevitably involves some risk. Some risk taking is healthy and a necessary part of growth. At the same time, it is important to manage the risks and do what you can to ensure the safety of everyone involved. These precautions not only help to protect young people, they also can help to protect your organization from legal problems.

It is important to keep in mind, however, that the best way to safeguard you and your organization against unnecessary risk is to design and implement high-quality, well-planned activities. The legal issues are only in place in case something goes terribly wrong. That's less likely when you've planned carefully. The bigger issue is ensuring that young people have a positive, safe, and challenging experience. You can provide these kinds of experiences by:

■ Asking service-learning veterans to share what they know about designing fun, effective, and safe programs;

■ Establishing and communicating clear guidelines, expectations, and policies (national organizations such as the Nonprofit Risk Management Center have resources and guidelines to assist you in developing your own policies); [8]

■ Keeping everyone involved informed and up-to-date about your activities;

■ Not trying to hide problems or concerns (better to delay a project or be overcautious than to have a minor problem turn into a real emergency);

■ Being honest about risks, but not overplaying them; and

■ Offering training and clear guidelines for leaders and participants.

 NOTE: *Be sure to check with your organization's leaders, attorneys, and insurers to ensure that your efforts comply with the specific needs and requirements of your organization, your state, and current law. The following information simply raises issues to address; it is not intended to be legal advice.*

Insurance—Policies differ in terms of what they cover and where. Your organization's policy may be fairly restrictive or broad enough to cover almost any activity you want to undertake. Find out if there is a policy in place and what it covers. If there is no policy, find out if you need one and, if so, how to obtain it.

Transportation—Service-learning often involves shuttling young people to, from, and around sites. Clearly communicate your safety expectations to everyone involved in transporting young people, including drivers, riders, and leaders. Worksheet 6 offers some transportation guidelines to consider.

Parent/guardian permission—Permissions slips serve as proof that parents or legal guardians are aware of opportunities presented to their young people and give permission for their children to participate. If you include additional information on the slip, such as the goals of the project and activities included, you can also help parents better understand some of the risks, content, and rationale of the program.

What's essential in a good permission slip? Apart from space for the participant's name and a parent's or guardian's signature, the following should always be included:

■ Name, location, and phone number of the site(s) where you will be serving;

■ Description of how you will get to and from the site;

QUESTIONS FOR SHAPING
YOUR TRANSPORTATION GUIDELINES

Consider the following questions in developing transportation guidelines for your service-learning efforts. Before adopting policies, check with organization leaders, attorneys, and insurance providers to ensure that your guidelines are appropriate for your organization.

Drivers

▶ Will you use only bonded or professional drivers, or will you include volunteers?

▶ Will you have an age limit (such as people over 21 years old)?

▶ If you allow youth to drive, will you have restrictions on how far or long their trips can be?

▶ Will parents have the option to specify adult-only drivers for their children?

▶ Will you do any background checks on drivers' records?

▶ Is the driver's own insurance coverage sufficient? Do you need a special organizational policy?

Vehicles

▶ What kinds of vehicles will you use?

▶ How many people are allowed to travel in each vehicle?

▶ Are standard seats and seat belts mandatory?

▶ Will you do any maintenance checks prior to using each vehicle?

Planning and Coordination

▶ Will you provide maps and directions?

▶ Are there plans for what to do in emergencies such as getting lost, having a flat tire, or being in an accident?

▶ Will medical release forms travel with the group leader or with individual drivers?

▶ Will drivers be alerted to any potential health or behavioral problems among their passengers?

Road Rules for Drivers

▶ Are all vehicles expected to travel together?

▶ Are drivers clear on their responsibility to follow speed limits and drive defensively?

▶ Will drivers have a list of young people in their vehicle?

▶ Are drivers responsible for keeping track of their passengers and making sure they get to and from the site?

▶ Are your drivers expected to model any particular behaviors?

Road Rules for Passengers

▶ What kinds of activities and behavior are and are not acceptable while traveling?

▶ Who makes decisions about music selections and volume?

▶ Will young people choose or be assigned to vehicles?

▶ Are they expected to travel both ways in the same vehicle?

■ Date and time of the activity (including departure and return times);

■ A brief overview of what you will be doing and why; and

■ Recommendations about what to wear and what to bring (food, money, tools, supplies).

Permission slips are more for parents' peace of mind than for protection for your organization. They indicate an *implicit* assumption of reasonable risk on parents' part, but it is important to note that they carry no weight in cases of negligence. Many institutions that work with children and youth use permission slips that have a waiver of liability clause. This clause has questionable value that may give leaders a false sense of security. Therefore, some experts recommend leaving it off permission slips. Consult your organizational leaders and legal advisers before deciding whether or not to include such a waiver on your permission slips.

Medical release forms—In medical emergencies such as illness or injury, every reasonable attempt should be made to contact parents or guardians before providing medical care. However, since this isn't always possible, program leaders should have some form of authorization for emergency medical treatment for young people. This is especially important when they are doing outdoor work or physical labor and in cases where a young person has a medical condition that may require quick attention (such as severe allergies or diabetes). A sample medical release form is provided in Worksheet 7. Before using this or any medical release form, consult a legal adviser.

Interpersonal relationships—One of the great opportunities in service-learning is to build relationships across generations. In most cases, those experiences are positive and enriching. But it is important to remember that someone who seeks to get involved in your effort may not have the best interests of young people in mind. A single incident of physical, emotional, or sexual abuse can deeply wound a

young person and destroy your service-learning effort. It is important, then, to take necessary precautions to keep young people safe in their relationships with adults who are involved in your service-learning program.

Most schools, youth-serving organizations, and agencies serving children and youth offer guidelines for protecting children and youth from abuse within their programs. Several national organizations (including Big Brothers Big Sisters of America, Boys & Girls Clubs of America, Boy Scouts of America, and Camp Fire Boys and Girls) offer guides, curricula, and other resources in this area.

In *Screening Volunteers to Prevent Child Sexual Abuse: A Community Guide for Youth Organizations,* the National Collaboration for Youth identifies specific factors that affect the level of risk within an organization or program, as well as ways to reduce the risk in each area.[9] The guide identifies the "Four Ps of Organizational Child Abuse Prevention":

■ **Personnel**—Managing risks related to staff and volunteers includes issues of screening, training, monitoring, and discharging personnel appropriately. A screening process discourages or deters people from getting involved in programs who would be risks, it can identify applicants who may be risks, and it can address concerns of parents and others regarding the safety of the young people involved.

■ **Program**—This area involves examining activities to identify areas of risk and taking steps to mitigate those risks. A primary strategy in this area is "to reduce the number of situations in which an adult volunteer and child can be isolated without others being present."[10]

■ **Premises**—If the setting for the program or project is not well-lit, does not have controlled access, or has private rooms and spaces, enhanced supervision may be appropriate.

■ **Participants**—One way to reduce risk is to train participants and their families, outlining clear expectations, rights, and how to deal with any concerns.[11]

WORKSHEET 7

SAMPLE MEDICAL RELEASE

To Whom It May Concern:

As a parent and/or guardian, I authorize a qualified and licensed medical doctor to treat the following minor in the event of a medical emergency that, in the opinion of the attending physician, may endanger her or his life, cause disfigurement, physical impairment, or undue discomfort if delayed. This authority is granted only after a reasonable effort has been made to reach me.

This release is intended for (date) _____. This release form is completed and signed of our own free will with the sole purpose of authorizing medical treatment under emergency circumstances in my absence.

Minor's Name: _____

Signed (mother, father, legal guardian): _____

Date Signed: _____

Street Address: _____

City, State, ZIP: _____

Daytime Phone: _____

Evening Phone: _____

Other Phone (cell, pager, etc.): _____

Insurance Carrier: _____

Policy Number: _____

Primary Physician: _____

Phone: _____

Medical allergies, medicines currently being taken, chronic illnesses, or other conditions: _____

_____

Another person to contact in case of emergency:

Name: _____

Daytime Phone: _____

Evening Phone: _____

Other Phone (cell, pager, etc.): _____

Taking necessary precautions to eliminate as much as possible the risks of inappropriate relationships is essential in service-learning efforts. At the same time, the asset-building perspective reminds us of the importance of looking for strong, asset-rich adults. The National Collaboration for Youth guide puts it this way: "Organizations should not focus only on negative elements when recruiting and screening volunteers to work with children. Look for good adult role models; individuals who demonstrate stability and have a healthy self-esteem. These individuals will be less likely to pose a risk of child sexual abuse."[12]

> **? QUESTIONS TO CONSIDER**
>
> ▶ What kinds of policies, expectations, and practices does your organization already have to create safe experiences for young people? How can you build on these?
>
> ▶ Who in your organization can you tap to assist in shaping policies and procedures for risk management and youth safety?
>
> ▶ How will you balance a healthy sense of caution in providing safe experiences with the inevitable risks involved in challenging projects and in relationships?

Forming strong adult-youth relationships is a key benefit of service-learning. By taking the time to manage and reduce the risks, you can increase the odds that all young people who participate will benefit from the positive, enriching, and lasting relationships that can form as adults and youth engage in meaningful work together.

Cultivating a Culture of Service

Service-learning projects can happen in an organization with no other service commitments. But if your goal is for young people to learn that serving others is a normal, ongoing part of life, it's important that helping others, generosity, and service become clear, normative expectations—not just for young people involved in projects, but for everyone in all areas of their lives.

You don't create a culture of generosity and service through programs, though they can certainly contribute to and reinforce such a climate. Some of the ways to be intentional in helping to create a culture of service within your organization include:

■ Having a clearly articulated organizational commitment to serving others. Tie service to your organization's core mission and purpose;

■ Encouraging leaders in the organization to be role models of serving others;

■ Expecting, encouraging, and inviting people of all ages—from young children to senior citizens—to serve others on a regular basis;

■ Having clear expectations that people help out each other, beginning at early ages. Encourage adults to invite children and teenagers to help them—even if it would be easier "to do it myself." This help can include everything from simple courtesies ("Could you please hold the door for me?") to inviting young people to be part of major projects;

■ Honoring the heroes—the young people and adults who inspire others to serve and make a difference in the world;

■ Ensuring that children and youth feel cared for in the organization. Young people who feel cared for are more likely to express caring to others;

■ Recognizing and celebrating small and large acts of kindness and service by many people in the organization and in the community; and

■ Having symbols of service and care visible in your organization's facility. These can include artwork, sculpture, stories, and other representations.

These ideas just begin to touch on some of the possibilities for creating a culture of service within your organization. Many organizations already have a history and tradition of service, and these kinds of actions only reinforce those traditions. For others, an intentional commitment to serving others may be new. In those cases, it is important to remember that nurturing this kind of culture can take years.

But the effort can be well worth it. This culture of service becomes a foundation for all your focused service-learning efforts. And it cultivates an institutional commitment to serving others that can be sustained through transitions and across time.

The Importance of Stage Design

In the theater, stage design is a fine art. A set designer must study a play carefully to determine what scenes are needed, the setting and period, backdrops, lighting, furnishings, props, sound, and dozens of other elements of the set. And while many theatergoers never notice many of those elements, they are critical to the overall experience.

In some ways, the tasks outlined in this chapter are like all the behind-the-scenes work that "sets the stage" for a dramatic production. Young people, parents, organizational leaders, and others may not notice many of these elements and the work that goes into putting them in place. But these foundational planning issues are essential to effective service-learning. They set the stage for young people to have positive, life-changing experiences that make a real difference in the community.

At the same time, no set would be worth creating if a play isn't going to be performed. So it's time to move to the four essential elements of service-learning experiences:

■ **P**reparation
■ **A**ction
■ **R**eflection
■ **R**ecognition

These topics are the focus of the next four chapters.

CHAPTER 5

PREPARATION: GETTING READY
TO SERVE

Chapters 1 through 4 emphasized service-learning as an ongoing commitment within an organization, not a one-shot project. The service, learning, and development goals for a service-learning program likely transcend multiple projects and multiple groups of people, and span several months or years.

Now it is time to focus on the steps involved in engaging young people in a specific service-learning project. Indeed, the remaining chapters of this book offer a process of preparation, action, reflection, and recognition that you can use over and over with different groups and different projects in your organization or community.

Preparation focuses on the key tasks in getting ready for a service-learning project. Involving young people in preparation is an essential part of the experience. Through this stage, young people:

■ Learn how to assess opportunities and needs;

■ Design a service-learning project in response to those needs;

■ Begin gathering the information they need to be effective as learners and contributors; and

☞ **A NOTE ON LANGUAGE:** *The material in this chapter and throughout the book assumes that the focus of service-learning is young people. If you are doing service-learning with families or intergenerational groups, they, too, need to be engaged in the process alongside young people.*

■ Develop the skills they will need to contribute effectively.

Setting Boundaries and Expectations for a Project

As you begin to plan and prepare for specific service-learning projects, it's important to set a context and parameters for the effort. Whom do you hope to engage in service-learning? Where will the service occur? What are your service, learning, and development goals?

These are the kinds of questions that were addressed in Chapters 2–4. They set some parameters on a specific project to ensure that it meets your goals and fits with your organization. Worksheet 8 can help you narrow the possibilities for a specific

---

? QUESTIONS TO CONSIDER

▶ How clear is your understanding of how service-learning fits with your organization and its priorities? How can you clarify issues before planning a specific service-learning experience?

▶ Is there a shared understanding among the service-learning planners of the boundaries and expectations you have for your service-learning efforts? If not, how can you build a shared understanding?

SETTING BOUNDARIES AND EXPECTATIONS FOR A SERVICE-LEARNING PROJECT

This worksheet summarizes some of the possibilities for service-learning projects that were discussed in Chapters 2–4 of this guide. Use it to come to a shared understanding within your planning group of the scope of your service-learning efforts.

Project Coordinator: _____

Planning Team Members: _____

_____

Whom do you hope to involve in the project?
(Check all that apply.)

_____ Elementary-age children

_____ Middle school youth

_____ High school youth

_____ Families

_____ Intergenerational group (age range: _____)

Where will the service take place?
(Check all that apply.)

_____ Within the organization

_____ In the community

_____ Within the state

_____ In another state: _____

_____ In another country: _____

How long will the service experience be?
(Check all that apply.)

_____ Short (1–2 hours)

_____ Half or full day

_____ Multiple visits (over an extended period)

_____ Intensive (weeklong trip, etc.)

How do you hope to build on your organization's mission and identity? _____

_____

_____

Any existing programs or activities to which you hope to connect the project: _____

_____

_____

What are your overall goals for:

Learning? _____

_____

Growth and development? _____

_____

Service impact? _____

_____

What available resources and relationships do you plan to tap? _____

_____

What funding sources will you use?
(Check all that apply.)

_____ Your organization

_____ Partner organizations

_____ Local service organizations or foundations

_____ Families and other allies

_____ Young people's own contributions

_____ Fund-raising

_____ Other: _____

What parameters will you place on the project to manage risks and ensure safety in terms of:

Insurance? _____

Transportation? _____

_____

Parental permission? _____

_____

Medical releases? _____

_____

Personal relationships? _____

_____

project. Use it to synthesize your thinking from the planning in the previous three chapters. Sorting out the choices before you actually start planning a project can help reduce confusion and misunderstanding. You may have to revisit your decisions, however, as you move into assessment and planning, since new possibilities may surface.

Narrowing the Service Options

Depending on the experience level, developmental stage, and readiness of the young people in your organization, you may not want to leave all the planning of a service-learning project up to them. You may want to build on the completed boundaries and expectations worksheet (Worksheet 8), and then do the assessment phase to identify specific project options for young people to consider. Depending on your circumstances, this approach can have several benefits:

■ It can give people a quicker taste of actual service experience, which can generate interest for more involvement in the future.

■ It reduces the risk that young people will want to do something that is beyond their capacity or that would cause controversy within your organization.

■ It may be necessary for projects in other states that require extensive contact with national or regional organizations that coordinate youth projects and work trips.

■ It reduces the chance that young people will get involved with an organization that doesn't have experience working with youth or that doesn't do effective service-learning. If that occurs, you risk having to do damage control from young people having negative experiences in serving others.

■ It allows for service involvement for younger youth who may not be developmentally ready to take on a long-term project.

At the same time, don't assume that you must always narrow the options. Your young people may

QUESTIONS TO CONSIDER

◗ What is the overall experience level of the young people who will be engaging in service? How much preplanning is needed to ensure that they don't get overwhelmed?

◗ How will you ensure that narrowing the options for service-learning experiences does not cut off the creative possibilities that young people might find particularly inspiring and meaningful?

have the maturity, passion, experience, and commitment to take on projects that you never would have dreamed of. In addition, you can work with them to identify projects that will be effective and that will have organizational support. Those are important leadership skills to learn.

Tapping Young People's Gifts and Interests

Young people play important roles in all stages of service-learning. But while organizational leaders may take the initiative in setting the stage (as outlined in Chapters 2–4), young people need to be nurtured as the actors and leaders throughout the service-learning process. Doing so is important for many reasons, including:

■ They are much more likely to be enthusiastic as participants.

■ Planning and preparation are critical elements of the learning process.

■ It reinforces a cultural shift from youth as recipients to youth as contributors.

■ Young people bring fresh ideas for solving problems.

In addition, many young people are already deeply concerned about social issues and want to make a difference. The 1995 Prudential Spirit of Community Youth survey of almost 1,000 high school students found that 95 percent of all teenagers "believe it is important for people to be involved in the community by volunteering their time to charitable, civic, cultural, environmental or political activities."[1] The challenge for service-learning leaders is to be catalysts for translating this general interest into concrete action.

Furthermore, young people's involvement in creating, planning, and executing a service-learning project has a direct effect on how the project affects them, according to a Search Institute study of the National Service-Learning Initiative and the Generator Schools—efforts managed by the National Youth Leadership Council. The researchers write:

Those [students] who worked as a group on both the planning and execution of the service experience were more likely to gain a sense of responsibility for civic involvement, were less likely to lose a sense of responsibility for helping others and for the environment, and were more likely to express the intent to serve others and be civically involved in the future. . . . The more personally responsible the youth are for their own service experience the greater the chance it affects them personally—assuming they reflect on the activities in a structured way.[2]

How do you get young people interested and involved from the beginning? Here are some possibilities:

Listen to them. Find out what they're interested in and passionate about. (Figure 11 shows the reasons young people give for volunteering.) Then find ways to translate those passions and interests into meaningful action through your general service-learning goals and priorities.

Invite them. Independent Sector asked teenagers how they first learned about their volunteer activities. The top methods were through school (42 percent), being asked by someone (40 percent), having a family member or friend who is already involved or who benefited from the activity (36 percent), and through participation in an organization or group or through the workplace (31 percent).

Only one in five (21 percent) sought out the volunteer activity on their own, and just 4 percent learned about the opportunity through an advertisement or printed request. In analyzing the findings, the Independent Sector researchers concluded that "volunteers are not made, but asked." Only 51 percent of all teens were asked to volunteer. Of those who were not asked, only 24 percent volunteered. Of those who were asked, 93 percent actually volunteered.[3]

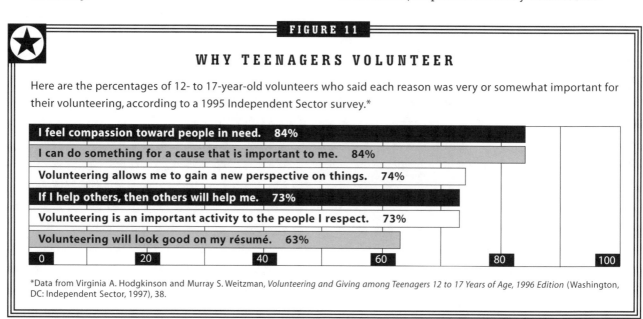

FIGURE 11

WHY TEENAGERS VOLUNTEER

Here are the percentages of 12- to 17-year-old volunteers who said each reason was very or somewhat important for their volunteering, according to a 1995 Independent Sector survey.*

I feel compassion toward people in need.   84%
I can do something for a cause that is important to me.   84%
Volunteering allows me to gain a new perspective on things.   74%
If I help others, then others will help me.   73%
Volunteering is an important activity to the people I respect.   73%
Volunteering will look good on my résumé.   63%

0   20   40   60   80   100

*Data from Virginia A. Hodgkinson and Murray S. Weitzman, *Volunteering and Giving among Teenagers 12 to 17 Years of Age, 1996 Edition* (Washington, DC: Independent Sector, 1997), 38.

Who should ask? Start with friends. Almost half (47 percent) of the teenagers who volunteered were asked by friends. Then came a teacher or other school personnel (31 percent), a family member or relative (31 percent), or someone in their congregation (22 percent).

Introduce them to people behind the issues. A powerful way to motivate young people to action is to introduce them to the people who are affected by issues. That's how students at Broad Meadows Middle School became advocates against child labor. Iqbal Masih, who was about their age, came to their school while he was in the United States to accept an award from a human rights organization. He told the students his story of being sold into bonded labor at age 4 because his parents owed a lender $12. For six years, Iqbal was chained to a loom, weaving intricate rugs. He escaped at age 10 and began to speak out about child slavery. The students later learned that Iqbal had returned to Pakistan and was murdered at age 12.

The students decided they had to do something. They started a fund-raising campaign to build a school in Iqbal's village. In letters that they sent all over the United States, they asked people to give just $12—the amount Iqbal's parents had owed the lender. They succeeded, and a $150,000 schoolhouse is now in operation, as well as other services. Furthermore, the middle school students continued their Kids Online March Against Child Labor, which seeks to get policy makers to enact tougher international child labor laws.[4]

Introduce them to service "heroes" or "giraffes." One way to inspire young people to get involved in service-learning is to introduce them to ordinary people who have made a major difference in the world. That's the philosophy of the Giraffe Project, a nonprofit organization committed to "finding, commending, and publicizing people who stick out their necks for the common good."[5] The organization collects stories of people of all ages and then uses storytelling as a way to inspire and motivate young people to action.

Whether or not you use the Giraffe Heroes Program for kids, you can use their basic idea. Who are people in your organization or community who could share their "hero stories" with kids? In religious communities, you can tap the stories of "faith heroes" in sacred writings or history. In youth organizations, you can tap the stories of the founders and activists who inspired the organization. In addition, young people can find and share their own stories of heroes.

As you begin focusing on specific issues or concerns, identify heroes who have addressed those issues. If you're working with an agency in the community, it would likely have staff or volunteers with a passion and commitment who would enjoy telling their own story in ways that would help young people see the possibility and potential.

A particularly powerful group of "heroes" are young people who have already had experience in service-learning. In telling their own stories and sharing their experiences, they help other young people catch the spirit, energy, and opportunity for growth, learning, and impact that service-learning can have. (Chapter 8 highlights ways to share experiences with others to continue the service-learning cycle.)

Make it personally meaningful and relevant. An essential part of building and maintaining enthusiasm is addressing concerns that are relevant and have meaning in young people's lives. For example, participating in a walk to raise money for and awareness about spinal cord injury research may not mean much to a group of young people who don't know anyone with a spinal cord injury. However, if a teacher or other person in the community has suffered a such an injury, it may be the ideal project.

Give them concrete ways to get started. If young people don't have much experience in service or service-learning or if they are younger, you'll want to start with simple opportunities for involvement.

They may not be ready to plan everything, but they can be invited to take on specific assignments or tasks. Over time, you can build on this initial involvement and engage them in more and more of the process.

Build on current commitments. Many young people may already be involved in some kind of service or volunteering, either on their own, with their family, or through another organization. How can you honor, celebrate, and build on those existing commitments?

Think outside the box. We often have preconceived notions of the focus of service and service-learning. We assume it has to involve a lot of kids, address particular kinds of issues, and take place in particular places. But some great service-learning possibilities emerge when you listen to young people and their interests without preconceived notions of how action will take place.

Take, for example, the Computer Service Club in the Dassel-Cokato area of Minnesota. Community leaders recognized that half of the teenagers in the area were not connected to organized youth programs. Some of these young people were technologically savvy. So the community formed the service club in which students solve people's computer problems at no charge. In the process, young people get to hone their computer skills while connecting to others in the community and being seen as a great resource for technology that frustrates many adults.[6]

Equipping Youth for the Service-Learning Process

It's one thing to give young people the specific skills they need to take action—using equipment, practicing the skills, and other specifics related to the work. In service-learning, young people also need to be equipped to be active in the whole process (PARR—preparation, action, reflection, recognition). They also need to be aware of the goals that guide the effort.

Process—If young people are going to play an active role in the whole service-learning process, they need to be equipped for each area of work. So if young people are involved in gathering supplies for a project, they need to learn skills for calculating needs, ordering materials, and keeping track of deliveries and inventory. If they will be doing fundraising, they need to know about how to engage in that process effectively.

Most of the processes involved in service-learning can be important learning opportunities. Some can be service projects in themselves. If, for example, young people gather information on available resources in the community (as part of the assessment process), that information may be extremely valuable to others working in the area.

Learning—Young people need to be aware of the learning goals that are in place to guide the selection and design of a service-learning project. If specific goals are not set, then consider inviting the young people to work with adults to set those goals in ways that interest the youth and meet the organization's mission and expectations.

Service—You should not settle on specific service

? QUESTIONS TO CONSIDER

▶ When have young people surprised you with the kinds of issues or concerns that motivate them to take action? What can you learn from those experiences?

▶ What are opportunities in your organization to listen to young people's hopes and dreams? How can you use those opportunities to begin identifying service-learning possibilities that would tap their passions and commitments?

▶ Who are some local "heroes," role models, or community members who could inspire and motivate young people to get involved in service?

goals until you have completed the assessment phase and talked with the community members who will be recipients of or partners in the service-learning process. However, the service parameters you established in setting the stage are important for young people to know.

Growth—If your service-learning efforts build upon the developmental assets framework, young people need to be familiar with the basic ideas in asset building. This will help them keep an asset focus when planning, and it will also help to guide the reflection process. It also emphasizes the role young people have as contributors to asset building.

You may want to use some of the information in Chapter 1 to introduce young people to asset building. An easy way to start talking about the assets with youth is to copy and distribute Figure 5. Explain that these assets are things that research has found that all young people need to help them be successful in life. Ask each young person to circle the assets he or she experiences. Then talk about which of the 40 assets are currently being built in your program or class, and how your service-learning activities might build even more of the assets.

In addition, Search Institute has produced a variety of tools that may be helpful in introducing assets to young people. They include:

■ *What Teens Need to Succeed* (Free Spirit Publishing, 1998)—a book for youth on what the assets are all about and how they can build the assets;

■ *Building Assets Together: 135 Group Activities for Helping Youth Succeed* (Search Institute, 1998)—a workbook with activities and worksheets to help young people learn about the assets; and

■ *Taking Asset Building Personally* (Search Institute, 1999)—a personal workbook and facilitator's guide for sessions designed to help youth and adults reflect on their own asset-building experience and opportunities.

Equipping young people with skills and information doesn't mean, however, that adult leaders need

---

> ## ❓ QUESTIONS TO CONSIDER
>
> ▶ For which parts of the service-learning process are the young people most prepared? Where do you see more of an opportunity to build skills, knowledge, and expertise?
>
> ▶ Are young people aware of the service, learning, and growth goals that have been established? What might be the most effective ways to share that information?
>
> ▶ Who in your organization might be able to assist in equipping young people for service-learning? Are there young people or senior citizens who have previously participated or who are active volunteers who could be mentors and guides?

---

to give a series of lectures. Rather, adults and other youth with experience can be coaches and guides in the process, offering just-in-time, on-the-job training throughout the process. In addition, several tools and resources are available to train young people in different stages of the process. This guide can be used by both youth and adult leaders. Many worksheets can be used to summarize information and teaching basic ideas.

Assessing the Current Situation

Assessment of issues, concerns, and needs in the setting where young people will serve is the first major step in planning a service-learning project. Taking time to assess community needs and priorities *with the community* has a number of benefits:

■ It ensures that the young people will do work that contributes meaningfully and that is neither patronizing to nor imposed on the community.

■ Young people set realistic goals and select opportunities that are more likely to be successful.

■ Community members are more likely to have buy-in to the projects that the young people take on.

■ Young people learn a great deal about community, social issues, research, and respecting people who are different.

■ It creates excitement and passion for the project as young people see, firsthand, how they can contribute to others.

If you work with a community agency, the agency may already have completed an assessment. Or it may be that gathering information on opportunities, priorities, concerns, and needs is the first project young people take on. The basic question to be answered is this: If a group of students were available to help solve problems and meet needs, what kinds of opportunities might there be for them?

There are many tools, strategies, and approaches for identifying issues and priorities in a community. One way is to direct contact residents (through

---

? QUESTIONS TO CONSIDER

▶ What experiences, if any, have you had in the past of identifying needs, priorities, and service opportunities with members of the community? What worked well? What was challenging?

▶ What benefits do you see in your organization to working with community members to identify priorities? How might this experience be different from other service projects you've done?

---

phone interviews, visits, surveys, etc.) to ask for their input. This approach can yield rich information, but it also tends to be fairly labor-intensive and requires significant skills. Another strategy is to ask agencies and leaders in the community for their perspectives on priorities and opportunities. In either case, it is important to report back to the people who shared information what you learned, how you plan to respond, and why.

If you want to tie the service your group provides directly to asset building, consider using the asset

framework as a tool for gathering information in the community. Use Worksheet Figure 9 to identify questions to ask and to gather information to help select your project.

As you gather information and select projects, find ways to have direct involvement by people in the community. This may include young people spending time in the site. Or, if you're planning an out-of-town project, the contact might need to be by phone. You can also invite community members to come to your school, organization, or congregation to plan with the young people. However, remember the value of spending time in the community where young people can actually see issues, people, and opportunities—and where people can introduce you to their world and be comfortable and safe in a familiar setting.

Identifying Possible Service Projects

You've set goals and parameters. You've identified the setting where you want to serve. You've identified needs and opportunities in that setting. And you've identified and cultivated young people's interests and passions.

It's time to pick a project.

It may be very clear exactly what to do, based on the information you've gathered. Or there may still be many possibilities. Consider first brainstorming as many possibilities as you can (and jotting all the ideas on newsprint).

There are many, many ways to organize project possibilities to help stimulate your thinking. Here are a few:

■ What project possibilities do the eight categories of assets suggest? Figure 12 gives a number of ideas.

■ What possibilities are there for indirect service, direct service, advocacy for change, or educating others? Table 6 gives suggestions.

■ What projects could young people initiate (such as organizing a neighborhood cleanup)? How might

IDENTIFYING NEEDS AND OPPORTUNITIES THROUGH THE ASSET FRAMEWORK

Use this tool with community members to identify possible types of service-learning projects that tie to each of the categories of developmental assets.

Asset Category	Examples of Possible Service Areas	What's Present? (Strengths to Build Upon)	What's Missing? (Gaps to Fill)
Support	▶ Strengthening families ▶ Building intergenerational relationships ▶ Mentoring ▶ Caring for homebound residents ▶ Meeting basic needs for food, clothing, shelter		
Empowerment	▶ Leadership development and training ▶ Addressing safety concerns ▶ Start-up help for gardening or landscape improvement		
Boundaries and expectations	▶ Addressing issues such as vandalism, alcohol and other drug use, graffiti ▶ Introducing children to positive role models		
Constructive use of time	▶ Building or repairing sports and recreation facilities ▶ Providing programs and activities for younger children ▶ Performing dance, music, and other art forms		
Commitment to learning	▶ Tutoring and other educational support ▶ Improving school facilities ▶ Reading and literacy programs (for all ages)		
Positive values	▶ Leading educational program related to values ▶ Advocating for social justice causes		
Social competencies	▶ Teaching conflict resolution or mediation skills to children ▶ Supporting cultural enrichment activities and celebrations		
Positive identity	▶ Start-up assistance for community-led activism ▶ Creating stories and histories of the people and places in the community		

FIGURE 12

ASSET-BUILDING SERVICE-LEARNING PROJECT IDEAS

Service-learning projects can build many of the assets in different ways. Here are some project ideas that relate to each category of developmental assets.

Support

▶ Deliver meals to people who are shut in and spend time talking with them while they eat.

▶ Start or join a tutoring or mentoring program for younger children.

▶ Start an escort or tour service for visitors to your organization.

▶ Lead recreation programs in a nursing home or day-care center.

▶ Form a welcoming committee that reaches out to children and youth who move into your neighborhood.

Empowerment

▶ Compile a list of service opportunities for young people in your community. Make it available to other organizations that are interested in service-learning.

▶ Coach sports teams for younger children.

▶ Write letters to local leaders about for how to make your neighborhoods safer for young people.

▶ Speak at public forums on issues that affect children and youth.

Boundaries and Expectations

▶ Develop a code of conduct for your organization and hold awareness-raising sessions to let all adults and young people know about it.

▶ Start a "Clean Up Your Act" campaign. When you see people in your neighborhood or organization acting inappropriately, tell them that you don't like what they are doing and would like them to stop.

▶ Pair adults and youth with similar interests and help them find a project in the community that they both want to work on.

▶ Host a seminar for families on the importance of asset building, including having family rules and consequences for breaking those rules.

Constructive Use of Time

▶ Start a theater troupe that goes to different schools and other organizations to raise awareness about issues such as exercise and nutrition, alcohol and other drug use, sexual harassment, or the importance of building assets.

▶ Offer an after-school activities program for younger children.

▶ Help build or repair a community youth center or other youth-friendly space in your community.

▶ Collect slightly used musical instruments and donate them to a local school.

Commitment to Learning

▶ Offer English as a second language tutoring for families in your community.

▶ Read or tell stories to younger children.

▶ Collect books for a juvenile detention center.

▶ Create posters for your school or organization that proclaim the importance of learning.

Positive Values

▶ Facilitate "Shared Values" discussions within your organization to identify values that are commonly held.

▶ Write letters to advocate human rights through an organization such as Amnesty International.

▶ Advocate for humane conditions for livestock.

▶ Help teach human sexuality to younger children.

Social Competencies

▶ Hold a talent show focused on cultural diversity. Include poetry readings, music, skits, and other expressions of one's own culture or the beauty inherent in a multicultural society.

▶ Develop a conflict management team.

▶ Start a peer-helping program in your organization. Train young people to be supporters and champions of one another.

▶ Create and distribute T-shirts and buttons with messages of tolerance and understanding.

▶ Develop a training program for younger children in how to resist pressure and avoid dangerous situations.

Positive Identity

▶ Organize a career fair for other young people in your organization or community. Invite adults from the community to talk about why they do the jobs they do, and how they got to the position they are in.

▶ Distribute voter registration information and campaign for candidates who reflect a positive vision of the future.

▶ Regularly send notes to friends and other young people telling them what's great about them.

they tie into existing projects (for example, helping to build a Habitat for Humanity house)?

■ What could individual youth do on their own or with a small group? What kinds of projects would require a larger group of youth?

Evaluating the Possibilities

Once you've brainstormed possibilities, begin narrowing the options based on the parameters in place. There are many ways to sort through possibilities. For example, you could start by having each person select two projects that they think would be best. Then the whole group could discuss those that generated the most votes in light of your parameters and goals. Worksheet 10 offers a checklist you could use to evaluate potential projects. Add other questions that are particularly relevant to your organization.

Once they've reviewed their options, young people can make informed choices about how and where to commit their energy. It will be clear from the evaluation which projects fit best with the many variables that contribute to an effective service-learning experience.

Keep in mind that you don't have to do just one project. If your group is large, you may be able to support multiple projects at the same time. If, for example, a particular project interests only a few young people, but enough to accomplish the goal, you may want to encourage them to take it on themselves. Or you can plan to do a series of projects that meet different needs and interests.

Planning the Project

Once you've committed to a project, you need to develop a plan and assign responsibilities. Worksheet 11 is designed to assist with key planning tasks. Depending on the scope of your project, this plan may include:

■ Working with other partners or a sponsoring agency;

■ Fund-raising;

■ Additional assessment and information gathering;

■ Identifying specific work sites;

■ Gathering needed supplies and tools;

■ Training young people with project-related skills;

■ Building awareness and support in your organization;

■ Recruiting additional youth and/or adults to participate;

■ Encouraging parental involvement and support;

■ Planning transportation; and

■ Addressing safety and risk issues.

It is also important to develop a plan to ensure that you achieve your goals in all three areas: service, learning, and growth and development. Indeed, one of the challenges in the service-learning field is that many programs do not have their intended or hoped-for results. A Search Institute study of middle school service-learning illustrates two common reasons that programs don't have their intended results:

■ **Duration**—In this study, most of the young people were involved in projects that lasted only about 10 hours. Previous research suggests that 20 to 30 hours of service are needed to realize the most positive effect on the young people.

■ **Reflection**—Structured reflection is clearly tied to positive impact, yet only 14 percent of the young people in these service-learning programs reported doing "a lot" of reflection. Half reported doing only a little—or none at all.[7]

So, in addition to planning the logistics of the service project, it's also important to build into the plan the kinds of reflection and learning opportunities that make it more likely for young people to grow through the experience.

Keep in mind that preparation should not be the responsibility of just the leader(s) of your program. In fact, it's usually much easier and more effective for training to be handled by people who are familiar with places you'll be serving and the tasks involved. People who might be called on to help with training include adults and youth who have prior service-

TABLE 6

BENEFITS AND CHALLENGES
OF DIFFERENT TYPES OF SERVICE

Service activities can take many forms, from indirect service you perform within your organization to hands-on involvement to education and advocacy. Use ideas on this chart to identify possibilities that fit with your group's priorities, resources, and interests.

Type of Service:	Examples	Benefits	Challenges
Indirect service: Activities that provide resources or services to others without any direct contact with the recipients	▶ Organizing a food drive ▶ Collecting blankets and winter clothing for homeless people ▶ Raising funds for organizations, causes, or disaster relief ▶ Preparing food for a shelter ▶ Creating care packages for new teen moms, refugees, or other groups in distress	▶ Meets important needs ▶ Can build connections to distant places in the world ▶ Does not require transportation	▶ Doesn't put young people directly in contact with recipients ▶ Can perpetuate stereotypes or an "us and them" attitude about people being served
Direct service: Hands-on action on behalf of people or issues	▶ Assisting an elderly person or someone with a disability with shopping or other household tasks ▶ Tutoring younger children ▶ Helping immigrant families practice speaking and writing in English ▶ Being a mentor to a younger child ▶ Working on home repairs or construction of affordable housing	▶ Provides opportunities for relationship building ▶ Can increase cross-cultural understanding ▶ Personalizes social and justice issues by connecting them to individual people ▶ Can offer immediate, tangible results	▶ Demands a stronger commitment from young people ▶ Typically involves multiple visits over time or a extended experience ▶ Usually requires transportation
Advocacy for social change: Speaking out on behalf of others and working to change the underlying conditions that keep them in need	▶ Sponsoring a voter registration campaign ▶ Working to educate potential and current voters about issues ▶ Writing letters to the editor or submitting articles about social issues to newspapers or other media ▶ Participating in boycotts of goods or services that exploit vulnerable populations and/or harm the environment ▶ Speaking up about social issues at town or committee meetings ▶ Working on behalf of individual policy makers or other leaders	▶ Highlights justice issues for young people, reminding them of the systemic conditions that can perpetuate injustice ▶ Gives young people experience in civic engagement and world issues	▶ Results almost never come quickly and may not be recognizable for years, if ever ▶ Issues can be divisive and solutions complex ▶ Some types of political involvement may be inappropriate for some groups
Education for change: Young people become catalysts for change by learning about social issues and sharing what they learn with others	▶ Develop a presentation about local hunger issues, HIV/AIDS education, or other themes ▶ Compile and distribute a list of easily accessible resources for families in distress ▶ Immersion opportunities where young people experience a different culture or setting in an intensive experience ▶ Participating in community events and celebrations that honor the richness in the community's diversity	▶ Builds young people's information-gathering and leadership skills ▶ Positions young people as resources in their community ▶ Provides the knowledge for young people to get more directly involved in issues and advocacy	▶ By itself, does not provide direct contact with people in need ▶ Can create conflict if issues are controversial

WORKSHEET 10

CHECKLIST FOR EVALUATING PROJECT POSSIBILITIES

Use this form with some possible projects to narrow possibilities and make choices. If you don't know the answers to some questions, you may want to find out before selecting a project.

Description of the Potential Project: _____

_____

	☺	☹	?
A. How well does the project fit with **your young people's:**			
1. Interests and passions?			
2. Developmental stage and ability level?			
3. Life experiences and other differences?			
B. How well does the project fit with **the community's:**			
4. Needs and priorities?			
5. Existing resources and programs?			
6. Experience and capacity in engaging young people in service?			
C. How well does the project build upon **your organization's:**			
7. Mission or purpose?			
8. History and identity?			
9. Current projects and programs?			
10. Leaders' commitments and support?			
D. How well does the project address **your goals** for:			
11. Learning?			
12. Growth and development?			
13. Service?			
E. Is the project appropriate for **your group's:**			
14. Size?			
15. Level of skill and experience?			
16. Time availability and commitment?			
F. Will you be able to adequately address **infrastructure issues** such as:			
17. Funding?			
18. Risk management and safety?			
G. Other:			
19. _____			
20. _____			

PROJECT OVERVIEW SHEET

Agency or Organization: _____

Contact Person: _____

Address: _____

Phone: _____

Fax: _____

Email: _____

Project Description: _____

_____

_____

Project Site/Location: _____

Participants:

Name	**Phone**
_____	_____
_____	_____
_____	_____
_____	_____
_____	_____
_____	_____

Transportation Coordinator: _____

Equipment and Supplies Coordinator: _____

Budget and Fund-raising Coordinator: _____

Project Schedule

Task	Date	Time	Location	Task Leader	Task Team Members
Preparation					
Action					
Reflection					
Recognition					

learning experience, individual mentors who are working with your young people, or staff or volunteers from the organizations you'll be working with. Remember that agencies have a vested interest in the young people being successful in the project, too. Worksheet 12 offers some questions to consider in deciding who should be involved in different parts of preparation and training.

Let's look at preparation in each of the three goal areas: service, learning, and growth.

Getting Ready to Serve

Planning the service component is primarily a matter of planning the action and ensuring that young people are prepared with the skills, knowledge, and sensitivities they need to be successful. There are several components of this planning:

Planning the action—What exactly will young people do? What are the various tasks and assignments? What supplies, if any, are needed? Is there a sequence of tasks that need to occur over time? These basic kinds of planning questions are an important part of preparation.

The amount of planning needed will vary considerably by project. If young people are going to a classroom of younger children for reading, for example, the planning would focus on scheduling and selecting books from the library. On the other hand, if young people are helping to build or refurbish homes, the action will involve many steps, from getting permits and supplies to doing the remodeling in the appropriate order.

If you take on a more complex service-learning project on your own, planning can be quite intense. Many schools, congregations, and youth organizations partner with an agency with expertise and experience in doing the project, so some of the details will already be in place.

Orientation to the site—Young people who have not been involved in selecting the project site will want to know what the site is like, what they are likely to encounter there, and whether or not they will be safe. The more they know about the site, the less orienting they'll need later on and the readier they will be to serve. An advance tour of the site is the best way to accomplish this, although photos or a video can be helpful if a tour is not possible.

If young people will be working in an organization or agency, tell them about the agency's mission, history, and program. If possible, introduce them to key people in the organization.

Orientation to the work—If they will be doing physical labor, young people will need to know what to wear, what supplies to bring, how to handle tools they will use, and so on. It's also a good idea to introduce them to any terms or concepts they might hear or use such as "paint rollers," "joint compound," or making something "level." A quick introductory session with a professional in the field they'll be working in can reduce the confusion and insecurity they might feel later on.

Skills building—Whether or not there are physical skills that young people will need to develop, there will likely be some interpersonal skills they need. As comfortable as they may be talking with family or friends, they may not know how to initiate a conversation with an elderly resident of a nursing home, a peer who is living in a shelter, or others they encounter whose language or lifestyle seems very different from their own.

Knowing who they are likely to meet in the course of the service, and having some conversation starters ready, can make the experience much easier. They may also need some direction on what questions not to ask or not to answer. Let them practice their new skills through some spirited role-playing in pairs or as a large group.

In addition, do not assume that young people understand appropriate conduct and etiquette in the setting in which they will be serving. Consider addressing the following questions:

■ What basic etiquette may be assumed to which the young people may not be accustomed?

■ How do people in the setting and those being served prefer to be addressed (Mr., Mrs., Ms., first names, etc.)?

■ If you're working with another agency, does it have specific rules or regulations that might affect the young people?

■ Are there cultural differences in terms of dress, language, gestures, and other customs that young people need to understand?

? QUESTIONS TO CONSIDER

▶ What are the major issues, concerns, or areas of discomfort that need to be addressed to prepare young people to participate in the planned service-learning experience?

▶ Are there types of preparation that can minimize the risk of injury or problems at a work site?

Orientation to different people and environments—One of the rich opportunities in service-learning is for young people to have experience in different settings or cultures. Preparing them in advance with information and opportunities to practice skills (through presentations, role-playing, videos, and other strategies) can nurture in them the confidence and skills they need to deal with these new (and sometimes intimidating) situations. Details about what they will *do* should be balanced with information about what they might *see* or *feel*.

Getting Ready to Learn

Intentional learning can be woven throughout the preparation, action, reflection, and recognition phases of the service-learning project. The ways you weave it into your efforts will vary considerably, depending on your learning goals and the young people involved.

For example, a clown troupe visit to the children's ward of your local hospital can be handled in many ways. At first glance, it could be a great way to break up the young patients' daily routine, unleash your young people's creative talents, and give them a chance to see that, behind the bandages and strange-sounding illnesses, all kids have a lot in common. Depending on how you approach it, the visit could also:

■ Serve as an opportunity for young people to think and talk about why some people seem to suffer more than others;

■ Act as a springboard for a dialogue on careers in medicine; or

■ Lead to a discussion of human rights and what health benefits should be available to all children, regardless of family economics or place of birth.

A service-learning project that focused on the first option would be quite different from one that concentrated on the second. The kind of facilitation needed from you or other program leaders would change dramatically.

Leaders can find many ways to enhance the educational aspect of a service project, says Maryanne Wonderlin, a service-learning coordinator in Louisville, Kentucky. A language arts teacher in the middle school in town chose plays and books with themes related to homelessness and aging, two areas of the students' service work. A science teacher did a section focusing on human growth and development—of added interest to students who were visiting children in day-care centers and nursing home residents as part of their service learning.

Worksheet 13 can be used to plan how you will integrate learning into each phase of the service-learning cycle.

Another part of preparing to learn is preservice reflection. Service-learning experts and trainers James Toole and Pamela Toole write: "Reflection *before* service may seem a contradiction, but we commonly reflect on and use prior knowledge and

WORKSHEET 12

COORDINATING TRAINING AND ORIENTATION ACTIVITIES

A classroom teacher or youth group leader may not always be the best person to offer training, orientation, and preparation for young people, particularly if several organizations and groups are involved. Indeed, all groups that are involved should share in the orientation and training. Use this worksheet to create a coordinated orientation plan among the various partners.

Training/ Orientation Topic	Who Will Lead It?	How Will Others Support It?	Where Will It Occur?	When Will It Occur?

PLANNING TO LEARN

Project: _____

_____

_____

Key learning objectives and curriculum tie-ins:

▶ _____

▶ _____

▶ _____

▶ _____

How will you intentionally address the learning objectives during preparation (e.g., studying a culture, researching related social justice issues, studying sacred writings, examining the history, geography, or economy of the area where you will serve)?

_____

_____

_____

_____

How will you intentionally address the learning objectives during action (e.g., specific knowledge that will be used or gathered)?

_____

_____

_____

_____

How will you intentionally address the learning objectives during reflection (e.g., reflection questions and methods that emphasize the learning objectives)?

_____

_____

_____

_____

How will you intentionally address the learning objectives during recognition (e.g., celebrate and highlight the learning that has occurred)?

_____

_____

_____

_____

▶ What are the different kinds of learning that could occur through the particular service experience? How will you guide the experience and reflection to fit with your learning goals?

▶ What kind of learning during the preparation phase might lay a foundation so that young people can learn even more as they participate in the service activity?

experience when we plan and design any project.... A critical component of preservice reflection involves students' examining the existence and source of their current attitudes and beliefs about immigrants, people with disabilities, the environment, or any other issue they face."[8]

Many of the reflection techniques outlined in Chapter 7 can be adapted for preservice reflection. A primary goal is to examine existing knowledge, beliefs, attitudes, and assumptions that young people bring to their service experience. Often, the Tooles write, this process of reflection and digging into deeper issues will reshape how the young people go about doing the service project.

Getting Ready to Grow

The whole service-learning experience—from initial assessment and preparation to final recognition and reporting—can be a growth experience for young people as they develop new skills, build new relationships, and form new perspectives on the world around them and their contribution to it. However, growth can be hindered if young people are not adequately prepared.

Debbie Loesch-Griffin, a service-learning evaluator, tells the story of a class of students who worked with a Head Start program. The students didn't relate well to the young children, didn't know how

to discipline effectively, and didn't know what were appropriate behaviors. So while the children and youth had some fun together, the young people's involvement added a tremendous amount of work for the Head Start staff who had to deal with the issues.[9]

Preparation in the following areas can help to encourage growth:

Establish clear expectations—Set explicit ground rules for how all participants are to interact with each other as well as with community members who are being served.

Build relationships—Depending on the nature of your group and the service being done, you may want to do some team building before you go to the work site. This can be particularly important if this group hasn't done much together, or if it's an intergenerational group that could slip into adult-focused leadership, not shared responsibility.

Introduce young people to challenges they may face—Many young people and adults can participate most fully when they are aware of some of the challenges and realities they may face during the service experience. This preparation not only can reduce anxiety (and thus make them more ready to learn and grow), it can also begin to address any prejudice or stereotypes that young people have. For example:

■ If young people are engaging in service in the developing world, they may never have been exposed to the kind of poverty they would likely see in a developing country such as Haiti.

■ If young people have never been around people with mental illness, they may need to learn what it's like to be with and communicate with people who are mentally ill.

■ If they have only spent time in an urban center, they may worry about the night sounds and darkness of a rural or isolated setting.

Introducing young people to the challenges can be done in many ways. Sometimes a video or speaker can prompt good discussion. In some cases, simulations, role-playing, and other experiential exercises can be helpful. There may be someone in the organization with firsthand knowledge who would be willing to work with the group. Or you could ask young people to investigate the issues and then share what they learn with everyone else.

> **? QUESTIONS TO CONSIDER**
>
> ▶ What kind of growth do you hope will occur through the service-learning experience? What can you do before the project to make that growth more likely?
>
> ▶ What kinds of issues, challenges, biases, or prejudices might get in the way of growth? How might you begin to address them before the action step begins?

In addition, you may want to help them anticipate problems and brainstorm ways to solve them. For example, what will you do if there is bad weather? If things don't go as planned? The point is not to make young people worry, but to help them anticipate and be flexible.

Preparing Adult Allies and Leaders

In the same way that young people need to be prepared for service-learning, the adults who work with them also need to be ready to serve. In many cases, adult allies and leaders benefit from participating in the same training and orientation as the young people—not just to prepare them, but also to build the relationships and shared experiences with the young people.

An additional area of training or preparation for adults is to equip them to be allies *with* youth, not leaders *of* youth. A key element of this training is to address the ways many adults undervalue youth,

take over responsibility from youth, or overprotect youth from failure. Barry Checkoway writes: "Adults . . . are sometimes insensitive to their own behavior in interactions with young people. Despite their best intentions, adults still tend to speak more often than young people, interrupt their sentences, frustrate their involvement, and cause them to withdraw from participation."[10]

One training option would be to talk with the adults about their roles as asset builders for the young people who are participating. The group could discuss questions such as:

■ How will we each work to create supportive, caring relationships with the young people?

■ How will we ensure that all the young people feel that they are valued and are contributing?

■ What is our role in setting and enforcing boundaries?

■ How will we help young people develop their own skills, values, and commitments?

■ How will we model positive values with the young people?

■ What skills do we have that we can help to nurture in young people?

If your group of young people will be working in an agency or setting that has not engaged young people before, it is important to talk with program leaders about appropriate ways to interact with and support young people. Too often, agency staff can have preconceptions about young people that interfere with young people's ability to contribute.

> **? QUESTIONS TO CONSIDER**
>
> ▶ How much experience do the adults who will work with youth have in serving as resources and supporters for youth, not directors and leaders?
>
> ▶ What specific issues do you expect will arise that will need to be addressed in training and preparing the adults who will work with the youth?

Preparing Parents

Parents can be important allies in your service-learning efforts—or they can be obstacles if they are suspicious, don't understand, or have many unanswered questions. They need to know what's going to happen, how it might affect their children, what's hoped to be learned, and how they can be supportive and involved.

Depending on your organization and the type of service you're doing, there are many ways to engage parents. If the project is short term and local, you may only want to inform parents about it and, if needed, get their permission to participate. If, however, the project is longer, out of town, or has higher demands, you likely will want to host parent information meetings, send information home with young people to parents, and identify specific ways parents can participate in and support the project.

? QUESTIONS TO CONSIDER

▶ What experiences have you had previously with parental support (or resistance) to youth activities or service-learning? What kind of preparation and parent involvement would those experiences suggest is particularly important?

▶ What opportunities do you already have to interact with parents? How can you use these opportunities to prepare them for their children's service-learning involvement?

In addition to the details of the service project, parents need to know about the other components as well. It's important to share with them the overall service, learning, and development goals for your effort, as well as an overview of effective service-learning. For example, you may want to introduce them to the PARR model and give them a copy of Table 2, Service-Learning Connections to the Eight Categories of Developmental Assets. You may also want to talk about asset building and how service-learning fits with this overall strength-building vision.

Finally, you can offer parents suggestions for how they can enhance their children's learning, growth, and experience at home. Figure 13 is a reproducible handout for parents that offers some suggestions for how parents can support their child's service-learning involvement.

Moving Ahead When the Time Is Right

Just as some people focus all of their energy on the action phase of service-learning, it can be easy to get stuck in preparation. Jumping into action can be scary or intimidating, but there is a limit to what you can do to get ready. Indeed, if you invest too much in preparation, young people will lose sight of the action phase and can lose interest and commitment.

At some point you have to move on, trusting that you have the most important pieces in place. The rest will come with time and experience.

FIGURE 13

SOME WAYS YOU CAN HELP YOUR CHILD GROW THROUGH SERVICE-LEARNING

Your child has the opportunity to participate in a service-learning project. Service-learning experiences combine opportunities to serve others while also learning and growing. This learning and growth occur as young people actively participate in four key elements of service-learning:

▶ **Preparation**—Selecting and getting ready for the service experience.

▶ **Action**—Making a meaningful contribution to others or the community.

▶ **Reflection**—Debriefing and learning from the experience.

▶ **Recognition**—Celebrating and assessing the experience.

Supporting Your Child's Involvement

As a parent, there are many things you can do to ensure that your child has a great experience of learning and growth. Here are ways you can support your child's involvement in service-learning:

▶ Encourage and affirm your child's involvement. Let her or him know you're excited about this opportunity and proud of how he or she will make a difference.

▶ Seek to understand the goals of the service-learning program or activity so that you can reinforce them at home.

▶ Talk with program leaders if you have questions or concerns.

▶ Volunteer to drive, provide refreshments, be an adult sponsor, or take on other responsibilities that fit your availability and schedule. Ask your child or a program coordinator about what kinds of involvement are needed.

▶ Talk with your child about her or his experiences, questions, insights, and beliefs. Share your own values and beliefs about the issues at stake, but don't overpower or dismiss your child's emerging thoughts and beliefs.

▶ If you have opportunities, take family excursions to places that build on or reinforce the service-learning experiences.

▶ If your child is participating in an extended work trip, encourage her or him to write letters or email telling you about the experience.

▶ Don't dismiss the idealism or deep commitment that often follow an intense, moving service-learning experience. Instead, find ways to reinforce and affirm the positive commitments and priorities evoked by the experience.

▶ Take time to participate in programs or events where the young people tell about and celebrate their experiences.

Encouraging Your Child to Serve Others

In addition to supporting a specific project in which your child is involved, there are many things you can do at home to help your child develop an attitude of service. Here are a few:

▶ Show care to your child. Children and teenagers are more likely to develop values of caring and service if they experience love and care from others. Find other adults to show care to your children, too.

▶ Make service part of your own life. Children are more likely to believe it's important to serve others if they see their parents modeling it.

▶ Talk about humanitarian and social justice issues at home. Think together about how you or your family might respond to these needs.

▶ Follow up on cues from your child. Often children and teenagers will get interested in a particular issue or need. These times can be wonderful opportunities to reinforce or solidify their commitments and sense of justice and compassion.

▶ Do projects together. Not only will you reinforce the importance of serving, you'll also have a lot of fun.

CHAPTER 6

ACTION: MAKING A DIFFERENCE

Although action is just one of four steps of service-learning, it is usually the most visible and tangible—and the one that gets the most attention. Action is important for what it does for others *and* for what it does in the lives of young people. Action has a wonderful way of moving social issues from young people's heads into their hearts and hands, and can serve as a real motivator for ongoing change in the lives of youth. After all the preparation and talk, young people are eager to actually *do* something about the important issues they have raised and discussed.

Action is most effective when it's preceded by comprehensive preparation and followed by effective reflection and recognition. Understanding action as an important step in the overall service-learning process will help you make the most of young people's service involvement and use it as a building block for further learning and reflection.

When you enter the action stage, it's not enough just to let it happen. There are several ongoing tasks that require attention. These include:

■ Nurturing an asset-rich experience for young people;

■ Establishing clear assignments, expectations, and schedules;

■ Keeping a focus on the learning and development goals;

■ Supporting young people as they serve;

■ Promoting interpersonal and cultural sharing;

■ Coping creatively with changes at the site;

■ Providing supervision and ensuring safety;

■ Keeping energy levels high;

■ Meeting ongoing training needs;

■ Keeping others connected; and

■ Documenting experiences and preparing for reflection.

The action phase varies considerably, depending on the type of project you're doing, where you do it, the age of the young people involved, the number of young people, and many other factors. So some of these tasks may be less or more important. For example, if you are planning a weeklong summer work trip for a dozen youth, the travel, lodging, and project logistics are very different than if you're arranging for two or three young people to serve every week in a local animal shelter. Thus, the details of how you accomplish each of these tasks (and how much energy you put into each) will depend on the specifics of your project.

Cultivating an Asset-Rich Experience for Young People

Almost by their nature, service-learning projects can be times when many developmental assets can be built or reinforced. But young people can also engage in service (itself an asset) without experiencing many other potential asset-building interactions and experiences. Being aware of possibilities can increase the number of ways young people can grow through the experience.

Also think about ways you can intentionally model asset building as you lead or coordinate a service experience. Figure 14 offers tips for reinforcing asset building during the action stage. In addition, several of the tasks that follow touch on specific categories of assets.

Consider keeping the list of assets with you during the project. It can remind you of ways you can build assets throughout the experience. For example, sometime when you really have the urge to yell at a young person, try giving yourself a five-second "time-out" by looking over the list of assets. You'll probably find that you calm down a bit and can turn the situation into an important lesson in peaceful conflict resolution (asset #36). Here are some other examples:

■ If a parent expresses concern or discomfort about the type of work taking place, you can encourage positive family communication (asset #2) by inviting her or him to the site to talk with you and the young person about safety and the precautions you are taking.

■ If your site is near a business area and your work is visible (such as making improvements to a local playground), you could increase asset #7 (community values youth) by inviting business people to a reception to unveil your completed project.

■ Keep relationship building as your number one priority. Since most of the assets are built through relationships, focusing on nurturing and encouraging them between youth and adult volunteers, youth and their peers, youth and agency staff or clients, and youth and younger children is a great step toward building all the assets!

There are other things you can do to help keep assets as the focus of your work. Even if you are very aware of the assets, others in your group may not be. Periodically check in with adults and young people to reflect on what assets they see being built and which ones seem to be missing. By talking and thinking about the assets regularly, you'll reinforce the idea that asset building is something to which everyone can contribute.

Establishing Clear Assignments, Expectations, and Schedules

Some of the common problems in service-learning experiences occur when roles, expectations, and assignments are not clear—or young people are given assignments that don't fit their developmental level. Thus, many service-learning advocates recommend developing clear job descriptions. The job description can describe the task, responsibilities, who is supervising, the work site, the time commitment and schedule, and the anticipated results.

In addition, it is important to be clear about schedule and time commitments. Agencies that typically use adult volunteers may need to adjust assignments so that they are appropriate for young people who might only be able to serve one or two hours per week for three months.

Finally, it can be important to share with young people clear expectations for their behavior and involvement. Figure 15 offers some suggested guidelines for young people built around the framework of developmental assets.

FIGURE 14

REINFORCING ASSETS DURING ACTION

Here are some ways adult leaders and allies can model asset building and create an asset-rich experience for young people during the action phase of service-learning.

Support

▶ Get to know all the young people who are serving.

▶ Encourage warm relationships between young people themselves, between young people and community members, and between young people and adult supervisors and servers.

Empowerment

▶ Ensure that all young people have meaningful roles and feel like they are really contributing.

▶ Monitor safety and enforce safety rules.

Boundaries and Expectations

▶ Have clear assignments, guidelines, and behavior expectations for young people.

▶ Encourage all adults and young people to model responsible, healthy behavior.

▶ Give young people assignments that are challenging but not overwhelming.

Constructive Use of Time

▶ Make sure that all young people have useful ways to use their time.

Commitment to Learning

▶ Keep the learning goals in mind. Point out connections between service and learning at the work site.

▶ Informally reflect on the experience during the project.

Positive Values

▶ Be honest with the young people, and expect them to be honest with you.

▶ Talk about issues of social justice that arise during the project.

Social Competencies

▶ Don't always just answer the questions or tell young people how to do things. Encourage young people to figure out some things for themselves.

▶ Encourage young people to get to know people who are different from them, even if it's awkward.

Positive Identity

▶ Let young people make mistakes and take risks (within appropriate boundaries). Help them learn from mistakes and then move on.

▶ Affirm and thank young people. Let them know they are making a difference.

FIGURE 15

EXPECTATIONS OF YOUNG PEOPLE DURING SERVICE

Here are some ways you can practice living the developmental assets as you provide service to others. We expect these kinds of behaviors from all young people who participate in service-learning projects.

Support

▶ Be courteous and friendly to others in the community, organization, and project.

▶ Get to know the people whom you are serving.

▶ Work cooperatively as part of your team to reach the goals.

Empowerment

▶ Take on meaningful jobs and tasks. If you don't feel like you're contributing, tell a program leader.

▶ Become familiar with emergency procedures at the work site.

Boundaries and Expectations

▶ Tell project leaders or staff when you cannot meet your timeline.

▶ Do not use language or dress in ways that might be offensive to people in the community.

Constructive Use of Time

▶ Be clear about your schedule. Be punctual.

▶ Don't waste time on the site; use your time (and other people's time) well.

Commitment to Learning

▶ Keep in mind your learning goals. Try to apply your knowledge to the situation.

▶ Ask questions about things that you don't understand or that make you curious.

Positive Values

▶ Be honest in raising issues and concerns that may arise.

▶ Treat everyone with respect.

Social Competencies

▶ Deal with conflicts that arise in healthy, peaceful ways.

▶ Ask for help in learning new skills that you need.

▶ If you're in a setting that's different from where you live, get to know the people and their culture.

Positive Identity

▶ Celebrate your contribution.

▶ Have fun!

Keeping a Focus on the Learning and Development Goals

In their classic guide to youth service programs, Dan Conrad and Diane Hedin quote from the journal of a student who was participating in a service project: "Today I went to a nursing home at 2:00. Talked to some ladies. Passed out popcorn at the movie. Went home at 4:00." That same entry occurred twice a week every week for the six-week duration of the girl's commitment.[1]

Young people can be doing great service, but that doesn't mean they are learning or that your development goals are being addressed. Some ways you can help to ensure that these goals are being addressed include:

■ Making sure everyone involved (adults, youth, agency staff) is aware of learning and development goals;

■ Talking with young people about what they are learning. Ask them questions such as, "How could you use what we've been learning in geometry to determine the angle needed to make that board fit?"; and

■ Encouraging young people to figure things out without just telling them.

Unexpected learning opportunities may also come up during the action phase. For example, young people may gain the trust of a caseworker at a family shelter and be given a chance to observe the intake process for a new family. Other options may be more informal, such as discovering that one of the elderly residents of a nursing home is a wonderful story-teller and gathering your group to hear what life was like before television and computers. Or an agency director may be willing to take time out of her day for a quick question-and-answer session or to offer her perspective on the needs of hungry or homeless people.

Learning opportunities may not relate directly to the agency you are working with, but rather to the neighborhood in which it is located or to the culture and traditions of the local community. They can involve thinking, tasting, listening, touching, and more. Each opportunity, no matter how small it seems, offers potential for enhancing the impact of service-learning.

As new options surface, assess how they fit with your goals and the needs of the agency and young people involved. You may choose to take advantage of some options and not others. What is most important to remember is that the unexpected may turn out to be the highlight of your visit. Be open to surprises and use them to your advantage.

Supporting Young People as They Serve

Effective action is virtually impossible without strong, supportive relationships between young people and the adults who are supervising and helping them. In addition, service projects that have people working side by side for a common purpose can be great relationship-building opportunities.

New surroundings and tasks are usually challenging and sometimes scary for young people. Regular instruction, guidance, and supervision will help them work through anxiety, apprehension, and nervousness they may be feeling.

In addition, it is important that young people know the adult leaders and allies care as much about *them* as they do about the tasks. You can convey this message in simple ways:

■ Learn people's names. Provide nametags for everyone involved, including service recipients.

■ Organize participants and leaders into work teams that are large enough to get the job done and small enough to foster relationships.

■ Be a model of support and encouragement for young people. Others will learn more from your actions than from your words.

One of the best ways to encourage young people is to catch them doing things well. This usually isn't too difficult during the action phase of service-learning. Take every opportunity to tell them *what* they are doing well and *why* their efforts are making a difference. Encourage young people to do the same for their peers and others they are working alongside, including agency staff, other volunteers, and service recipients.

Promoting Interpersonal and Cultural Sharing

Action, especially direct service, can help young people develop assets #33 (interpersonal competence) and #34 (cultural competence) by bringing them into contact with people who are different from them in terms of race, ethnicity, economic or social status, age, or in other ways. They also may have opportunities to educate others about their own situation or background.

These kinds of interactions can lead to an awareness that the things that make people different also make them special and interesting. They can also perpetuate stereotypes and misperceptions. For example, if your group is working in a homeless shelter, you may encounter people who have chemical use problems. If your youth have been part of programs or classes that teach that drugs are bad, they may get the idea that some people are homeless because of drug use and therefore it is their own fault and they don't deserve others' help.

You cannot—and should not—completely control whom your young people meet during service-learning. However, you can pay attention to the interactions they do have and make the most of them by doing some on-site reflection or making notes about issues to discuss later.

Coping Creatively with Changes at the Site

Regardless of how well you think you've planned and prepared, things are bound to change—especially when you are working at a new site. It's surprising the number and type of things that can go wrong in social-service agencies, such as:

■ The person you've worked with most closely and has planned to lead a facility tour and introduction is suddenly called away to deal with a client emergency.

■ Supplies ordered last month and guaranteed to be on-site last week were never delivered and no one on staff noticed because they were busy with other things.

■ The job you thought would take a day is finished before lunch.

Things can go haywire on your end as well, such as an unexpected flat tire, other transportation trouble, or a sudden emergency or event that leaves you with fewer leaders, drivers, or youth than you expected.

In the event that something does happen, first look for creative approaches to handling them (such as enlisting the help of a parent or other volunteer to shuttle groups of kids to the site and another person to work on getting the flat tire fixed). In addition, alert agency staff as soon as you know of the change, and keep in contact with them as you try to work things out. They may be counting on you to get important work done, so it's best to keep them informed. They should also keep you informed if they are working on problems on their end.

Hopefully nothing major will get in the way of your service. Contact the agency several days before you're scheduled to start, to confirm your arrival time and clarify your expectations about what will happen and the kind of work you'll be doing. Call again on the day of the event to confirm your arrival time and make sure everything is still on track.

If problems do arise, however, here are three ways to minimize hassles:

■ Find out as much as you can about the changes *before* you get to the work site. Let young people know about the problem and ask them to help you brainstorm solutions. Sometimes unanticipated changes make for better experiences. Other times, it's better to postpone the project than set yourself and your youth up for disappointment and frustration.

■ If changes are last minute and you're already on the site, make the most of what you've got. If the changes mean you can't do any work or have a delayed start, use the time for a discussion about the unpredictability of life, the challenges facing agencies with limited resources, or the struggles facing the people served by the agency. You could also rearrange your schedule to include a tour of the facility or neighborhood, or have a discussion with an agency staff member, volunteer, or client.

■ Realize that the group will reflect your attitude. The more positive you can be about the situation, the more your group will get out of it. If you approach it creatively, they will, too. If you are negative or resentful, it may taint the experience and their general attitude toward service.

There are times when certain sites or activities don't work out for some individuals or the group as a whole. If it is a one-time or short-term project, you may all decide to make the most of it by juggling jobs so that everyone shares equally in the ups and downs. This will work best with young people who have had other, positive service experience and are

confident in their ability to handle the situation.

If, however, your young people have little service experience or the project simply can't be salvaged, it is best to move on. Service-learning is not something to endure; it is a tool for learning and growth. Young people may learn valuable lessons when things go wrong, but that's no reason to stick with a bad situation longer than necessary.

QUESTIONS TO CONSIDER

▶ When have you participated in a service-learning project and something went wrong? How did people respond? What was the outcome?
▶ What can you do to model a positive attitude when things don't go as planned?

Providing Supervision and Ensuring Safety

Safety and security on the site should be top priorities. Young people (and adults) can sometimes get so caught up in a project that they don't realize how much they are stretching their bodies, minds, skills, or emotions beyond their limits. In addition, agencies that work primarily with adult volunteers may not know when their expectations exceed what young people can do safely and effectively.

Establishing clear guidelines and boundaries is the first step in safety. Some areas or tasks may need to be declared off limits. Issues to address may include:

■ Safety concerns in the area or neighborhood where the service is being done that require rules such as where young people can go alone, where they need to be with an adult, and where they should not go at all;

■ How much physical labor young people are expected to do;

■ Weather issues, such as heat, cold, or severe conditions;

■ Handling power tools, working on ladders or scaffolding, or other equipment issues;

■ Interacting appropriately with clients or other people in the community; and

■ Transportation safety.

There is more to supervision than safety, though. While young people may not want people constantly watching over their shoulders, they are usually more comfortable knowing that help and support are available. Check in with them regularly, especially if they are working individually or in small groups. Let them know how to contact you if they have questions or need something. As they gain more confidence and experience they'll need less assistance and more support.

Supervision also includes serving as the initial contact person if a young person raises a concern or issue, and being a liaison between young people and agency staff. This doesn't mean that young people shouldn't talk directly to agency staff, but it is a good idea for you to be aware of these interactions and serve as mediator in case of a problem. It may be easier for staff to have a designated person to deal with. In many cases, the agency you are working with will assign a particular person to assist

QUESTIONS TO CONSIDER

▶ What are the biggest safety risks involved with your project or program? What steps can you take to minimize those risks?

▶ Do you have enough adult staff and volunteers to adequately supervise the number of youth involved? If not, how could you get more adults involved?

▶ Who are the young people about whose safety you are most concerned? What about these people makes you nervous? What extra precautions can you take on their behalf?

you. If it hasn't, raise the issue yourself—before questions arise.

Keeping Energy Levels High

Sometimes when youth imagine service they think it is going to be exciting, heroic, challenging, and even fun. The reality doesn't always live up to these ideals. Scraping paint loses some of its appeal when muscles get sore and the sun starts to heat up the day. Important as they are, repetitive tasks such as weeding row upon row of a community garden or washing hundreds of dishes in a shelter will eventually get boring.

Even when young people have enthusiasm for the job, fatigue begins to set in when projects last all day, all week, or longer. To keep their energy up, most people of any age need rest breaks and enthusiastic encouragement. Rest breaks can take many forms:

■ Snack or drink time;

■ A chance to relax and rest, congratulate one another on the progress made so far, and set realistic goals for the remainder of the day;

■ An opportunity to check in with members of the group who are working on different tasks; or

■ Trading jobs partway through the day to use new muscles or skills.

There are also things your group can do to have fun even when things aren't going so well. Encourage your group to laugh at themselves and funny things that happen. Make the most of the light times, even in the midst of working on serious issues.

Meeting Ongoing Training Needs

No matter how extensive your preparation has been, young people will inevitably find themselves in situations they don't know how to handle. It may be something as simple as understanding which terms to use to refer to different aspects of the work you are doing. Other skills—such as agency procedures or how to handle equipment—may require structured training.

Some ongoing training needs that aren't urgent can be addressed off-site if your young people will be making multiple, regular visits and need to master several tasks. In this case, you can break their training into segments. Address topics that are most relevant to upcoming tasks. The training will be most effective if young people have the opportunity to put their knowledge into action *soon*.

In addition to formal training, encourage everyone involved in your projects to share techniques, ideas, or suggestions informally throughout your service experience. This can happen as you are working, during break times, or between visits. Pair less experienced people with those who have already mastered certain tasks, and encourage anyone who has discovered a faster or easier way to get things done to share the discovery.

Keeping Others Connected

One way to ensure that families, friends, and others in your organization are excited about and supportive of your service-learning efforts is to keep them informed about what you're doing. Making the effort to keep people informed not only helps keep conversation going with the young people who serve, it also strengthens support for your program and can inspire others to serve, too. The ways you stay connected will vary, depending on whether the project is local and ongoing or a work trip to another community, state, or country.

Here are some ideas for staying connected if the project is in your own community:

■ Include periodic updates (with photos) in newsletters, special mailings home, email messages, or a Web site.

■ Have young people give progress reports to gathered groups.

■ Create a bulletin board with photographs, illustrations, a map, and other symbols of the work.

■ Invite families and others to visit the work site—or help out one or more times.

Here are some ideas for staying connected if your group is traveling out of town for an intensive service-learning experience:

■ Encourage young people to write letters home.

■ Put regular updates (including photos) on a Web site, and encourage people to visit the site daily.

■ Give people maps and an itinerary so that they know where the group is.

■ Send home a video from early in the trip.

No matter where your service takes you, keep families and your organization informed by sharing your success stories and struggles through newsletters, letters, open discussion sessions, and presentations.

Documenting Experiences and Preparing for Reflection

Young people will get the most out of their service-learning if they have ways of documenting their experiences, learning, and questions throughout the process. Insights gained during action can too easily be lost in the return to a daily routine. Giving time and attention to documentation and reflection in the midst of action will help ensure that the experience has a lasting impact. There are many ways to promote reflection during the action stages:

■ Ask young people questions about what they are doing and why, what they are learning, and what they are confused or concerned about.

■ Encourage young people to write down any key words or phrases that describe their experience, their feelings, or what they are learning.

■ In group projects, assign young people to be the official photographers and/or videographers.

■ Encourage them to keep journals.

■ Arrange for young people to write about their day while they are at the site. The closer in time to the event, the more likely they will be able to remember what it was like and their thoughts and feelings.

■ If you are traveling to and from the site together each day, use the time to discuss the day's events and experiences.

■ Build in time at the end of the day to see how everyone is feeling and talk about any issues that came up during the day.

■ Keep your own notes or a journal to capture your reflections for later sharing.

Two excellent tools for documenting and reflecting on service-learning experiences are journals and portfolios. Here are some ideas of how to organize these tools.

Journals—Thought-provoking questions help youth reflect on their experience through writing, drawing, and taking pictures. Time for journaling, writing, and sharing can be built into your gathered sessions as well as encouraged as an at-home, follow-up activity.

Individual journal writing can also be complemented by a team journal that draws on everyone's reflections and is intended for sharing. While personal journals may not be appropriate for public sharing, a team journal can be a powerful tool for helping people understand the important issues young people faced through service-learning. Figures 16 and 17 are samples of two practical tools for helping young people journal. These were designed for high school youth who took part in an intensive, weeklong project. They can be adapted to meet your group's needs.

Portfolios or scrapbooks—A service-learning portfolio is a collection of items that help track the growth and development of a service-learning project and the people involved. Portfolios can be developed by a team, individuals, or both and may include photos, drawings, notes and letters, learning-session outlines, journal pages, worksheets, menus from lunch stops, and other important "artifacts" from your experience.

A portfolio can focus on the things young people learned, contributions from all participants and supporters, the people served, and/or the agencies worked with. Putting together a portfolio can help your team:

■ Clarify what was done and how;

■ Link instruction and action;

■ Connect values with real-life issues and experiences;

■ Trace changes in how you think about and respond to the issues and people you meet along the way;

■ Celebrate obstacles encountered and overcome;

■ Showcase the range of your talents and abilities;

■ Recognize your growth as a team that works together;

■ Grow in your writing and communication skills;

■ Identify what is meaningful and valued to you as individuals as well as a group; and

■ Share what you learn with the wider community.

While much of the compiling of the portfolio and reflecting on its contents will take place after the action phase, you will need to be collecting things along the way. It will help if you have a central location for storing items or if each young person has a folder or box. Encourage everyone to be on the lookout for interesting, unusual, or significant symbols of your experience.

FIGURE 16

ON JOURNALING

A journal is different from a diary. Diaries keep track of what's going on around you. Journals help you reflect on what's going on within you. Keeping a journal is like carrying on a continuing conversation with yourself.

Journaling can be a doorway to growth. Through journaling you can get more in touch with what you really believe and feel about what's happening around you. It can help you get to better know yourself, your world, and your values.

How do you start? Journaling involves just two simple steps. First, set aside a bit of time each day. Second, let what's in your head and heart flow. What you write doesn't need to be deep or profound or earth-shattering. It just needs to be you!

New service-learning experiences can provide you with lots of material. Write about your day's experiences and your reactions. Jot down the sights and sounds, tastes and smells, experiences and feelings that came your way today, and lingered on.

If you think of something to write about during the day and you don't have time to make a full entry, pull out your journal or scribble a quick note to yourself—jot down a few key words that will help you recall the thought or feeling. Journals are a great place to pack away thoughts for later on.

If you think best in sentences and paragraphs, write that way. If key words and phrases work for you, do that. And, if your mind connects best with color and line, draw your way to a successful journal.

Finally, remember that journaling should also be fun and relaxing—and make it so!

FIGURE 17

CONNECTING SERVICE AND LIFE

Here are questions that can spark ideas for writing in your journal and creating your portfolio.

Connecting with Experience

▶ Look back on today. What struck you most strongly? What happened?

▶ What images stand out in your mind? What sights and sounds and smells? What experiences and conversations? What was it about those images that made you remember them?

▶ What was happening in your heart? What did you feel? Upset? Surprised? Confused? Content? What touched you most deeply today? Why?

▶ What did you find most frustrating? Most hopeful? Why?

Connecting with People

▶ Look back on today. Who did you meet and work with during the day? Who did you relate to most easily? Who did you find it hardest to talk with? Why?

▶ What did you learned about the people you met? How are their experiences most like yours? How are they most different? How would you feel if you had to change places for a week? For a year? For a lifetime? Why?

▶ What did you learn about yourself today? What do you like about what you learned? What do you dislike and most want to change?

Connecting with Issues

▶ What was happening in your head? How did the experience change or challenge your convictions and beliefs?

▶ What needs did your service involvement try to meet? Why did or didn't it succeed?

▶ How were justice and injustice present in the situations you faced today? Did you learn anything new about what causes suffering? About what you can do to make things better?

▶ How are you part of the problem? Part of the solution?

Connecting with Your Learning

▶ What information or skills did you learn today?

▶ How did you apply knowledge and information you had learned before this project?

Connecting with the Future

▶ What did you learn today that will help you in your service work in the future? What needs to change in the world to make things better? What needs to change in you?

▶ What hopes and expectations do you have for those you served? For yourself?

▶ Did the service experience affect what you think you deserve from life? How you would like to live? What type of job or career you might choose?

CHAPTER 7

REFLECTION: MINING
MEANING FROM EXPERIENCE

Community-service-learning projects are potentially wonderful "textbooks." They involve complex problems, real-life contexts, and exposure to people who possess wide expertise and resources not found in schools. Both the challenge and strength of such textbooks is that they come without chapters, footnotes, labeled pictures, list of key concepts, and review questions at the end. If students are going to learn from service, it will not be instant or effortless. They will be required to organize and construct their own understanding from the rich content embedded within these experiences. . . . For this reason, no activity is more central to understanding and implementing service-learning programs than reflection.[1]

This quote from service-learning experts and trainers James Toole and Pamela Toole of Compass Institute in St. Paul, Minnesota, captures the importance of reflection in service-learning; research reinforces it. For example, a five-year Search Institute study of the National Service-Learning Initiative and the Generator Schools—efforts managed by the National Youth Leadership Council—found that young people are more likely to report positive outcomes when their service-learning experience includes intentional reflection. Furthermore, when reflection is low or absent, there are some undesir-

able impacts. For example, young people who didn't reflect were more likely to develop negative views toward serving others.[2] Other studies have found that college students who engage in structured reflection said they "worked harder, learned more and were more intellectually challenged than in regular classes."[3]

Thus, being thoughtful and intentional about reflection is as important as taking effective action. Reflection allows young people to think about, discuss, and make sense of the issues, ideas, and information they examined and experienced. It is the process through which you can frame the experience in light of your goals for learning and growth.

This chapter first focuses on reflection for young people's learning and growth, highlighting both methods for reflection and a process for reflection. The final element of the reflection process is assessing the project and your service-learning program, identifying what went well, what didn't, and what to try the next time. The chapter concludes with several tools for informal program monitoring or assessment.

Linking Reflection with Learning Goals

The focus, scope, and methods of reflection can vary widely, depending on your organization and your goals for service-learning. For example, the reflection process for a classroom of students studying biology will be very different from the process used by a group of 6 to 10 young people from a congregation involved in a Bar/Bat Mitzvah or confirmation service project. The biology students might focus on water quality, life cycles in the wetlands, or similar issues. The congregational youth group might study the responsibilities of people of faith to care for creation and respect for all of nature.

The key to the whole process, then, is to be intentional about designing reflection processes that focus on meeting the goals you established—both for your broad service-learning efforts and for your specific project. (See Chapters 4 and 5.) Those learning and development goals will shape your reflection activities, methods, and questions.

In schools, much of the content of service-learning can tie directly to classroom content, whether it is history, social studies, economics, or other topics. But those content-specific areas are not the only connections to formal learning goals. Consider the following examples:

1. Many forms of reflection involve authentic writing projects through which students can work on expressing their thoughts, learnings, and feelings clearly and concisely. James Toole and Pamela Toole write: "Service-learning uses writing as a tool to produce, not reproduce, knowledge. Students fill what are variously called learning logs, reflection logs, or thinking logs, with the constructive interplay between the core classroom content and their own personal reflections."[4]

2. Some reflection projects may involve writing, speaking, or developing some other skill to share learnings with others.

3. Students' personal experiences with an issue can motivate or guide them to examine related issues in social studies, history, biology, or any other related topics. This reflection could also include examining literature with related themes.

4. The arts (including industrial arts) can be a highly effective tool for reflection as young people seek to express and communicate what they experienced and learned through various media.

In short, the reflection process can give opportunities for young people to develop their academic skills in the context of experiences that are motivating and concrete.

When to Reflect

Reflection can be part of the entire service-learning process. During preparation, young people reflect on their previous experiences and attitudes connected to the service area. They also reflect on their own hopes for their involvement. However, that learning will be more limited, since young people's curiosity and motivation to learn will be fueled by the experience of service.

During the action phase, young people share their experiences, ask questions, solve problems, and learn from each other. Also critical during the action phase is to document the experience through journaling, a portfolio, photographs, videos, or other forms that can be used to remind young people of the experiences later.

Depending on the nature of your action, reflection can be integrated throughout the experience. If, for example, you are taking action across several weeks, you can design reflection activities for in between the action. If you're having a more intensive experi-

---

? QUESTIONS TO CONSIDER

▶ When have you seen young people really learn from an experience-based learning design? How can you build on those experiences and examples?

▶ What challenges do you foresee in making reflection an ongoing part of your service-learning efforts? How can you address those challenges?

ence, reflection can occur at the end of each day. In other cases, you may have to do the bulk of the formal reflection after the service is completed.

Whenever possible, plan for some reflection as soon after action as possible, when impressions and questions are still fresh. This is especially important when young people are new to service-learning or when a project has a high emotional impact.

Whom to Involve in Reflection

The bulk of the reflection processes will involve the young people (or intergenerational group) that engaged in service. Keep in mind, though, the possibility for reflection for other key stakeholders as well. Consider opportunities for:

■ Community members to reflect with the young people about the experience and the larger issues at stake;

■ Parents to reflect on their perceptions of their young person's involvement and their own experiences; and

■ Program leaders and adult allies to reflect not only on their service involvement but also on their role with the young people.

In addition, many other people may be brought into the reflection process as resources. These may include community members and leaders, activists and experts in particular issues, leaders in your organization (such as a clergy person who could be a resource for a youth group exploring the theological or spiritual dimensions of the experience), and many others. Keep in mind, of course, the importance of developing the reflection experiences to fit the diversity and developmental stage of the group involved.

If your service-learning experience has been for families or for intergenerational groups, be particularly aware of the tendencies for adults to dominate conversations. Also be aware of dynamics that may surface between parents and their children. While these dialogues can be challenging to lead (particularly when people don't have a lot of experience in

intergenerational dialogue), the benefits can be tremendous in terms of new understanding and deeper relationships.

Ways to Reflect

Reflection can take many different forms, depending on the type of action, the learning and development goals, and the age and experience level of the service participants. In writing about reflection, James Toole and Pamela Toole build on the idea of different forms of literacy, noting that "the person who is less comfortable in a small-group discussion may make a wonderful video documenting his community garden project for the food bank. The person who can't quite find the right words to write in her journal may draw a series of political cartoons that forcefully capture her experiences in a homeless shelter."[5] Figure 18 offers 40 ideas for methods of reflection.

It is important to select the type of reflection carefully, since it will shape the thinking and learning that occur. In addition, you will likely select several forms of reflection for a project so that all young people can participate fully.

For example, the Maryland Student Service Alliance's *Special Education Service-Learning Guide* offers suggestions for planning service-learning activities around six different themes: environment, literacy, poverty, senior citizens, substance abuse, and teaching tolerance. One of the proposed activities for teaching tolerance is to sponsor a schoolwide poster contest on diversity in the school or community. It then outlines four types of possible reflection:

■ Writing an article for the school newspaper;

■ As a group (or in cooperative groups), assessing the contest's effectiveness (Did it attain the goals? How could we do it better?);

■ Making a display of photos of students working on their posters; or

■ Discussing what students thought about while making their posters.[6]

FIGURE 18

40 WAYS TO REFLECT

Reflection on service can happen in many different ways. Select methods that fit your particular learning and development objectives, the age and skills of your group, and the available time and resources.

1. Complete guided worksheets on the project.

2. Create a bulletin board display.

3. Create a fund-raising campaign to provide financial support that builds on the service.

4. Create a journal.

5. Create a scrapbook.

6. Create a video or slide show.

7. Create a Web site on the topic.

8. Create an individual or group portfolio.

9. Create briefing papers for policy makers.

10. Create collages representing the experience or the issue.

11. Create drawings, paintings, or sculptures.

12. Develop and present a drama, puppet show, dance, or music concert.

13. Do a conference or workshop presentation.

14. Do public speaking about the project.

15. Role-play.

16. Draw editorial cartoons or comic strips.

17. Give oral reports to the class or group.

18. Have a "talk show" about the service project or the social issues involved.

19. Hold class or group discussions.

20. Host discussions with community members or experts.

21. Lead a school assembly.

22. Lead a worship service (for congregation-based groups).

23. Participate in a group simulation experience.

24. Plan a training session for other youth.

25. Plan the next activity the group or class will do together on the same topic.

26. Prepare booklets on related topics to be used to teach others.

27. Read and discuss children's books on the service topic or social issue.

28. Read articles or chapters on the social, religious, ethical, historical, or political issues at stake in the project.

29. Research social issues related to the project.

30. Study sacred writings, literature, or historical material related to the project.

31. Teach material to younger children.

32. Testify before a decision-making or policy-setting group.

33. Write a group letter to families suggesting how they can get involved together.

34. Write a letter to a parent or friend about the experience.

35. Write a letter to the editor of a newspaper.

36. Write about a specific topic.

37. Write an essay or report about the needs.

38. Write and illustrate storybooks to read to younger children.

39. Write articles for a local or organizational newsletter or newspaper.

40. Write poetry about the experience.

▶ What forms of reflection seem most comfortable within your organization? How effective do you think those forms will be for reflection on service?

▶ What are the different learning styles of the young people who participate in your service-learning efforts? What mix of reflection methods will invite all these young people to reflect in ways that tap their learning styles?

Or suppose an intergenerational group from a congregation helped build homes with Habitat for Humanity. Some possible types of reflection might include (depending on the learning and growth objectives):

■ Reporting to the congregation about the experience;

■ Having dinner or a picnic with the family that will be living in the home and listening to their hopes, dreams, and life experiences;

■ Studying scriptures together related to homelessness and the responsibilities of people of faith to address the issue;

■ Hosting a dialogue with local elected leaders to discuss problems of affordable housing;

■ Having small-group conversations about working together across generations; and

■ Creating a plan for maintaining contact with and support for the family that will be moving into the home.

Effective Group Reflection

While both individual and group reflection play important roles in service-learning, there can be particular value in having participants reflect on the experience together. Group reflection activities will be more effective if you plan carefully, use a variety of techniques to prompt conversation, and create an environment that is both safe and comfortable for young people. When safety and comfort are combined they create the ideal environment for the kinds of personal disclosure, philosophical exploration, and group cohesiveness that give reflection sessions richness and sincerity.

A safe environment—Safety has to do with knowing that your thoughts, feelings, and opinions will be heard and respected. Reflection will be a waste of time unless young people know that other members of the group are open to what they have to say, and that what they share will be handled with respect. Setting appropriate boundaries together establishes mutual agreement about them early on. It usually works best to let the group brainstorm its own boundaries. Here are some to consider:

■ Treat each group member with respect. Everyone has something unique to offer and deserves to be heard.

■ No put-downs or personal criticisms.

■ Speak for yourself and no one else.

■ If you don't understand what someone is saying, ask for clarification. Don't jump to conclusions or make assumptions.

■ Focus on finding solutions, not just talking about problems. Look for what's working, not just what is going wrong.

■ Respect the differences in how people express their thoughts and feelings.

■ Ask others for their opinions.

■ Honor everyone's right not to talk.

■ Listen more than you talk.

■ Take responsibility for yourself as well as the group. Support and reach out to others.

■ Keep everything said in the group confidential unless you are told otherwise.

As a leader, your role isn't to give answers, but rather to guide the exploration of questions and keep the group on track. Having clear boundaries and pointing out when those boundaries are violated will encourage a process that helps young people make sense of their experiences.

A comfortable environment—Picture a quiet, cozy room that's not too hot and not too cold, with comfortable chairs, a thick rug on the floor, no clock on the wall, soft lighting, and a table loaded with beverages and snacks. Imagine that it's big enough to move around and mingle in, but small enough to feel homey and hospitable. Add some quiet background music and you've got the optimal environment for an engaging group discussion.

That's not much like reality for most people. So rather than trying to find an ideal place, focus on the basics to create a comfortable space where young people want to relax, spend time, and be creative. As much as possible, do the following:

- Eliminate or minimize distractions. These can include passersby, phones, fax machines, and pagers.
- Try to find comfortable seating arranged so that all can see and hear one another.
- Provide snacks (or have snacks available for purchase).
- Make sure there is a restroom nearby.

Group size—Reflection is most effective in groups of 10 to 12. Small groups make it easier to build trust among participants and increase the likelihood that everyone will have an opportunity to share. Effective reflection can happen in slightly larger groups if young people already know each other well and have relationships of trust and respect. One way to deal with a large group is to begin and end the session together, but spend most of the time in smaller teams.

Effective process—Reflection requires an inviting, well-guided group process that honors the perspectives and experiences of all participants. Otherwise, it can degenerate into debate, individuals can dominate the discussion, or participants may only address superficial issues and give the "right" answers.

Service-learning expert Harry Silcox emphasizes

the need to encourage dialogue, not discussion. "In discussions," Silcox writes, "the participants present their views, give opinions, and make statements. In dialogue, there is a nondirective openness, a readiness to suspend opinions and a willingness to see and mentally 'play with,' the other person's point of view."[7]

QUESTIONS TO CONSIDER

▶ What are the potential benefits of using group process for reflection in your organization? What challenges do you foresee?
▶ What skills do you need to develop in group facilitators to ensure that they can effectively lead group reflection about the service experience? How will you nurture those skills?

A Process for Reflection

The field of service-learning often views itself as a type of "experiential education"—learning that begins with concrete experience. This field has developed extensive knowledge on what is important in the process of learning from experience. One of the leading theoreticians is David Kolb, who developed the experiential learning cycle shown in Figure 19. Service-learning expert Kate McPherson simplifies the language by adding three questions:

- *What?*, which focuses on experience;
- *So what?*, which focuses on meaning; and
- *Now what?*, which returns the focus to experience.[8]

In addition to allowing young people to move from concrete experiences to more abstract ideas and learning, following the experiential learning cycle invites people with different learning styles to participate fully in the process. Use Worksheet 14 to develop your own plan for reflection on a particular experience.

1. What? Looking back on the experience (reflective observation)—Begin with an opportunity for young people to piece together their experience and their feelings about it. Encourage them to examine what happened within them and around them, as individuals and as a team. The following sequence can help young people begin to learn from their experience:

■ *Start with the senses.* Begin reflection by inviting young people to talk about their sensory experiences —what they saw, heard, felt, smelled, and so on.

■ *Remember what happened.* Invite young people to reconstruct their experience, recalling the planned and unplanned things that happened, both serious and humorous.

■ *Identify the feelings.* Much of the power of service-learning lies in its effectiveness in helping youth identify what they felt, what prompted the feelings, and how they dealt with their feelings.

A key to effective reflection on the experience is the way you ask the questions. When trying to stimulate discussion, get young people started on their journals, or guide some other reflection activity, use open-ended questions that encourage extended, thoughtful responses.

2. So what? Interpreting the experience (abstract conceptualization)—Once young people have reflected on their experiences, they are ready to interpret that experience and formulate new concepts out of that experience—to find broader meaning. It is during this phase that the experiences are brought into dialogue with social trends, experts, classroom learning, literature, religious teachings, or other information that is relevant to your learning and development goals.

A helpful way to think about this part of reflection is to remember the three Rs of reflection:

■ **Reality** means the big picture of what conditions are really like. A little background research can provide statistics and stories to help young people understand the breadth of the situation and how many people it affects.

■ **Reason** is helping young people make the connections between what they have observed and the

reasons for larger social issues: the roots, causes, circumstances.

■ **Response** includes exploring what is being done to deal with the problem and its causes.

Worksheet 15 is designed to help young people keep track of the three Rs related to their issue or concern. You can also use it to frame a discussion or to guide young people in their personal reflection in their journals, portfolios, or other reflection projects.

This part of your reflection will likely include a focus on values, both personal and collective. Values such as caring for others, equality and social justice, integrity, honesty, and responsibility (assets #26–#30) are important to explore during reflection. There may be other values that need addressing as well. An exploration of values can be fostered in a number of ways:

■ Incorporating questions about values and beliefs into journal assignments, reflective handouts, and group discussions;

■ Researching the mission and other philosophical foundations of your organization that reflect particular values;

■ Asking a leader or panel of people from your organization or community to lead a session on putting your values into action;

■ Introducing young people to print or video resources that focus on values such as civic engagement or volunteerism;

■ Inviting agency staff and others you worked with to join you for a discussion of the values that underlie the work you have done and the issues explored;

■ Working together to create a visual image (such as a poster, mural, painting, or sculpture) or a story, play, poem, or song, of what your community would look like if everyone agreed to and lived by the values you are exploring; and

■ Exploring the values that challenge the idea of working together for the common good. Examples of these values include look out for number one, nice people finish last, and you can't fight city hall. Discuss

FIGURE 19

DAVID KOLB'S EXPERIENTIAL LEARNING CYCLE

Here are the four phases of David Kolb's experiential learning cycle, with some sample questions to prompt discussion about each phase.

1. Concrete Experience—Participating in a direct, immediate experience.

2. Reflective Observation (What?)— Examining the experience in light of beliefs, values, and previous knowledge:

▶ How would you describe to a blind person what you saw upon first entering the site?

▶ List four sounds or noises that you heard on-site.

▶ How did your sense of touch play a role in your experience of service?

▶ Write two sentences about the smell(s) of the place.

▶ How did people respond to you at the site when you first arrived and then as you were leaving?

▶ Write a brief paragraph about someone you met on-site.

▶ What did you feel when you first walked in the door? Why do you think you felt this way?

▶ What was the most important thing you did today? Why?

▶ What were you most pleased about? Why?

▶ What surprised you? Why?

4. Active Experimentation (Now what?)—Testing or applying the learning or concepts in new situations:

▶ Describe a personal conviction or belief that was strengthened by your experience.

▶ What else can you do individually to respond to what you have experienced and learned?

▶ How can we encourage other people to get involved in this issue?

3. Abstract Conceptualization (So what?)—Identifying ideas, concepts, and new learning that organize the experience and its meaning:

▶ What's one thing you learned about yourself?

▶ How does what we did relate to what we have been studying? How has what you've been learning in class help you understand or respond to the issues?

▶ How are things in our community or for the people we served? Why are things the way they are? What can be done to make the situation better?

▶ What is being done to help the situation? Is it working? What else could be done? Who is responsible?

▶ What are two questions that you'd like to ask the agency you served or the people you worked with?

Based on David A. Kolb et al., *Organizational Psychology: An Experiential Approach* (Englewood Cliffs, NJ: Prentice-Hall, 1979); and Glen L. Gish, "The Learning Cycle," in Jane C. Kendall and associates, *Combining Service and Learning: A Resource Book for Community and Public Service*, vol. 2 (Raleigh, NC: National Society for Experiential Education, 1990), 198–205.

PLANNING YOUR REFLECTION PROCESS

Service-Learning Project Name: _____

Goals	(Build your reflection process and questions based on your goals. See Chapters 4 and 5.)
For service	_____ _____
For learning	_____ _____
For growth and development	_____ _____

Reflection Process	**What reflection methods will you use (discussion, writing, projects, etc.)?**	**What key questions will guide the reflection at each stage?**
What? Looking back on the experience (reflective observation)	_____ _____ _____ _____ _____	_____ _____ _____ _____ _____
So what? Interpreting the experience (abstract conceptualization)	_____ _____ _____ _____ _____	_____ _____ _____ _____ _____
Now what? Exploring the possibilities for change (active experimentation)	_____ _____ _____ _____ _____	_____ _____ _____ _____ _____
Now what? Getting ready for the next time (assessment)	_____ _____ _____ _____	_____ _____ _____ _____

WORKSHEET 15

SORTING OUT THE THREE Rs

Often when you provide service to others, the issues that underlie the need are complex, difficult to understand, and sometimes overwhelming. Use this worksheet to help you keep track of the information you gather to help you understand. It focuses on three areas: Reality, Reason, and Response. Jot in the space provided the key points you learn in each area.

The issue you're investigating: _____

_____

_____

Type of Information   **What You Learn**

Reality—What's really hap-pening in the world related to this issue, beyond the slogans, statistics, stereotypes, and simplistic answers? How widespread is the issue or problem? What's its real impact? How did you see these realities through your service-learning experience?

_____

_____

_____

_____

_____

_____

_____

_____

Reason—How did things get to be like they are? What are the causes? What's the history of the issue?

_____

_____

_____

_____

_____

_____

_____

Response—What is being done to address the need or problem and its causes? What seems to be working most effectively? What are things individuals can do to con-tribute to the solutions?

_____

_____

_____

_____

_____

_____

_____

why these values are or are not present in your organization or community.

As part of your growth and development goals, you may also want to have young people connect the experience to asset building—both in terms of how they experienced assets and how they may have been asset builders for others. Figure 20 offers questions you can use related to each of the eight categories of developmental assets.

3. Now what? Exploring the possibilities for change (active experimentation)—This final phase is about integration of learning so that it can shape the future. This integration can take many different forms:

1. Whole-group (or subgroup) interest or commitment to follow through with ongoing service or activism to continue addressing the issues—and thus continue the service-learning cycle with new activities.

2. Commitments by individual students to address issues or concerns on their own or in a different setting.

3. Reassessment of learning and development goals to determine how well they were met and how to build on and reinforce the progress (through future projects or other activities).

Depending on the type of action your group has done, young people may have developed strong opinions about the kinds of change they would like to work toward. It also may have clarified for them some of their personal values. On the other hand, they may feel more confused about what they believe, or frustrated because they don't know how else to change a condition or problem that seems out of their hands. Guided reflection can help them find effective ways to act on their values and convictions.

An important component of the "now what?" phase of reflection is for young people to explore how they will internalize a commitment, attitude, and "habit" of serving others and contributing to the community—not just through formal programs but in their daily lives, their vocational choices, and their

> **QUESTIONS TO CONSIDER**
>
> ▶ How do you see this reflection process fitting into your organization and its structure?
> ▶ What phases of the reflection process seem most challenging? What can you do to increase your comfort level with those areas?
> ▶ What kind of training or support do leaders in your organization need to facilitate reflection?

families. Part of the "now what?" conversation can help young people examine what kinds of support, guidance, and encouragement they might need to maintain their commitment.

4. Now what? Getting ready for the next time (assessment)—The final task during reflection is assessment. Service-learning pioneers Dan Conrad and Diane Hedin identify three types of assessment in service-learning:

■ Assessing young people's **individual performance,** which is particularly important in schools. Conrad and Hedin suggest that students' written work, group discussions, individual conferences, and input from supervisors are all possible sources of information for assessing student performance.

■ **Formal program evaluation,** which may be important when the program is supported by external funding. If you need a formal program evaluation, seek the services of a professional evaluator with experience in the field.

■ **Program monitoring,** which focuses on the effectiveness of the program or activity itself, and brainstorming ways to improve it.[9]

Program monitoring or assessment can be intimidating, particularly when it is viewed as a measure of success or failure. However, it is well worth your time and energy, since it can:

■ Affirm the value of what you have done;

■ Build solid organizational backing for your work;

■ Strengthen existing program; and

FIGURE 20

USING THE DEVELOPMENTAL ASSETS TO GUIDE YOUR REFLECTION

If you are including discussion and learning about the 40 developmental assets as part of your service-learning program, here are some questions that can help your young people view situations through an "asset lens." It will help young people to have a list of the assets to refer to when thinking about these questions.

General Asset Building

▶ What assets did you see being built today for yourselves and for the people around you?

▶ Who were the most important asset builders at the work site? What made them such good asset builders?

▶ What assets were most missing from your experience?

Support

▶ Who were your biggest supporters today? What did they do that made you feel supported?

▶ Who did you support today? How did it feel to be an asset builder for someone else?

▶ How did what we did today make a difference in how supportive young people in our community (school, neighborhood, organization) will feel in the future?

Empowerment

▶ How safe did you feel on the work site? What would have made you feel safer?

▶ Why do you think our work today will make adults in the community think of young people in a different way?

▶ Did you feel valued and appreciated while you worked? Why or why not?

Boundaries and Expectations

▶ Did everyone who participated in our project behave in ways that you thought were appropriate? If not, what were some of the inappropriate things you saw? (Note: Ask students to just talk about behavior, not individuals.)

▶ Do you think we should have had more ground rules about what was OK and what wasn't? Why or why not?

▶ Who were the best role models at the site? Were they mostly adults? Young people? Volunteers? Staff?

Constructive Use of Time

▶ Did you do anything today that felt "creative"? Explain.

▶ Did your experience today make you more interested in getting involved in a youth program? cocurricular clubs or organizations? a congregation? another organization?

Commitment to Learning

▶ Did our work today make you interested in learning more about any particular subjects or topics? Which ones? Why?

▶ Did our work make you feel good about our school (organization, congregation)? Why or why not?

▶ Why do you think nurturing a commitment to learning is important? Wouldn't it be just as good to just do service?

Positive Values

▶ What values were you acting on today?

▶ Which values did you see reflected in the people (staff, clients, volunteers) you met at the site?

▶ Asset #27 is valuing equality and social justice. Is that a commonly held value in our community? What do you see happening that makes you think that?

Social Competencies

▶ Did being prepared for our work make it successful? Why or why not?

▶ Did you encounter people today who seemed very different from you? What was that like?

▶ Did anyone pressure you today to do anything you didn't want to do? How did you handle it?

Positive Identity

▶ Did anything you did today make you feel powerful? Explain.

▶ Did anything make you feel powerless? Explain.

▶ Did your service experience introduce you to any career ideas or interests that you hadn't thought about before? Which ones?

- Surface opportunities for trying new ideas or addressing other interests.

Thinking of program monitoring as an additional opportunity for reflection and as an opportunity to learn and improve can reduce the anxiety. It might be helpful to see your program assessment in much the same way as you view asset building for young people. Start with the program's strengths (its assets). Then look at what could be better (its asset potential), and what should be eliminated altogether (its deficits).

Worksheets 16–25 offer a variety of tools that you can use or adapt to gather information from program leaders, participants, agency or organizational partners, and others. You can combine the information from each of these groups to give a more complete picture of your program's strengths and growth areas. Here is an overview of the tools:

- Worksheets 16–25 offer open-ended questions to gain feedback from the different stakeholders in the project: program leaders, program participants, partner agencies and organizations, community members, and parents of program participants.

QUESTIONS TO CONSIDER

- What kind of assessment or monitoring will be most useful to your organization?
- How can you use the information from the assessment not only to improve your service-learning efforts but also to build additional support for service-learning among young people and in your organization?

These tools can either be filled out on paper, or the questions can be used for interviews or small-group discussions.

- Worksheet 21 offers a tool for assessing your project in light of the benchmarks found in a set of principles of effective practice for service-learning.
- Worksheets 22–24 focus on assessing your efforts in light of the developmental needs of elementary-age children, young adolescents, and older adolescents.
- Worksheet 25 can be used to gather feedback on the young people's experience through an asset-building lens.

WORKSHEET 16

ASSESSING YOUR SERVICE-LEARNING PROGRAM: A TOOL FOR PROGRAM LEADERS

Project or program title: _____

Leader or coordinator: _____

What were your goals for this project? _____

_____

_____

_____

_____

How well did you meet those goals? _____

_____

_____

_____

_____

What three parts of the project would you do differently next time? Why? _____

_____

_____

_____

_____

_____

What three parts of the project would you repeat next time? Why? _____

_____

_____

_____

_____

Which assets did your project build for your young people (including those that were part of your goals)?

_____

_____

_____

_____

Other comments: _____

_____

_____

_____

WORKSHEET 17

ASSESSING YOUR SERVICE-LEARNING PROGRAM:
A TOOL FOR PROGRAM PARTICIPANTS

Project or program title: _____

Leader or coordinator: _____

Why did you participate in this service-learning project?_____

_____

_____

_____

_____

_____

Are you glad you participated? Why or why not?_____

_____

_____

_____

_____

What three parts of this project were most important to you? Why?_____

_____

_____

_____

_____

What three parts of this project were least important to you? Why? _____

_____

_____

_____

_____

Will you participate in other service-learning projects in the future? Why or why not? _____

_____

_____

_____

_____

Other comments: _____

_____

_____

_____

WORKSHEET 18

ASSESSING YOUR SERVICE-LEARNING PROGRAM:
A TOOL FOR PARTNER AGENCIES AND ORGANIZATIONS

Project or program title: _____

Leader or coordinator: _____

Why did you get your agency involved in service-learning with youth? _____

_____

_____

_____

Did you have any specific goals related to this involvement? _____

_____

_____

_____

How well did you meet those goals? _____

_____

_____

_____

What surprised you most about the experience? Why? _____

_____

_____

_____

What pleased you most about the experience? Why? _____

_____

_____

_____

What frustrated or disappointed you most about the experience? Why? _____

_____

_____

_____

Will you participate in youth service-learning projects in the future? Why or why not? _____

_____

_____

_____

Other comments: _____

_____

_____

WORKSHEET 19

ASSESSING A SERVICE-LEARNING PROGRAM: A TOOL FOR COMMUNITY MEMBERS

Project or program title: _____

Leader or coordinator: _____

What did you hope would occur through this project in your community? _____

_____

_____

_____

_____

Did this project meet real, important needs in your community? Explain. _____

_____

_____

_____

_____

What three parts of the project were most important to you? Why? _____

_____

_____

_____

_____

What three parts of this project were least important to you? Why _____

_____

_____

_____

_____

If a similar project were proposed in your community in the future, how would you like it to be similar to or different

from this project? _____

_____

_____

_____

_____

Other comments: _____

_____

_____

_____

ASSESSING YOUR SERVICE-LEARNING PROGRAM: A TOOL FOR PARENTS OF PROGRAM PARTICIPANTS

Project or program title: _____

Leader or coordinator: _____

How were you involved with or connected to this project? _____

_____

_____

_____

_____

What did you hope your child would gain from her or his participation? Explain how those hopes were met or unmet.

_____

_____

_____

_____

How well did you feel informed about the project, its goals, schedules, expectations, and other issues? _____

_____

_____

_____

_____

What were the most useful ways information was communicated to you? The least useful ways? _____

_____

_____

_____

_____

If your child were to participate in a similar project again, what would you hope would be the same? What would you hope would be different? _____

_____

_____

_____

Other comments: _____

_____

_____

_____

_____

ASSESSING YOUR SERVICE-LEARNING PROGRAM
IN LIGHT OF THE PRINCIPLES OF EFFECTIVE PRACTICE

The following items reflect the 10 principles for effective service-learning that were developed at a Wingspread Conference in October 1989. How well did your service-learning effort fulfill each of these principles?

How well did the service-learning project	Very Well	OK	Not Well
1. Engage young people in responsible and challenging actions for the common good?	❑	❑	❑
2. Provide structured opportunities for young people to reflect critically on their service experience?	❑	❑	❑
3. Articulate clear service and learning goals for everyone involved?	❑	❑	❑
4. Allow for those with needs to define those needs?	❑	❑	❑
5. Clarify the responsibilities of each person and organization involved?	❑	❑	❑
6. Match service providers and service needs through a process that recognizes changing circumstances?	❑	❑	❑
7. Receive genuine, active, and sustained organizational commitment?	❑	❑	❑
8. Include training, supervision, monitoring, support, recognition, and evaluation to meet service and learning goals?	❑	❑	❑
9. Ensure that the time commitment for service and learning is flexible, appropriate, and in the best interests of all involved?	❑	❑	❑
10. Involve diverse populations?	❑	❑	❑

ARE YOUR SERVICE-LEARNING EFFORTS APPROPRIATE FOR ELEMENTARY-AGE CHILDREN?

Rate your service-learning opportunities for 6- to 9-year-old children, using the following scale: 1 = poor, 2 = fair, 3 = good, 4 = excellent. Then identify areas of strength and improvement, and strategies for change.

1 2 3 4   Children are involved in selecting service themes and activities.

1 2 3 4   Children can see immediate, tangible results from their service-learning activity.

1 2 3 4   Larger projects are broken into smaller tasks that children can complete without becoming overwhelmed or disinterested.

1 2 3 4   Children are challenged to grow through the service activities, but they are not challenged beyond their capabilities (reading, strength, height, etc.).

1 2 3 4   Children have opportunities to interact with adults, youth, and/or their families through their service-learning experience.

1 2 3 4   Service-learning activities offer a variety of options for participation, based on interests, abilities, and attention spans.

1 2 3 4   Children can participate in either group or individual projects that contribute to the overall activity.

1 2 3 4   The activities provide enough structure, direction, and focus for children not to be overwhelmed by too many choices or too much freedom.

Strengths _____

_____

_____

_____

_____

Areas for Improvement _____

_____

_____

_____

_____

Strategies for Change _____

_____

_____

_____

_____

ARE YOUR SERVICE-LEARNING EFFORTS APPROPRIATE FOR YOUNGER ADOLESCENTS?

Rate your service-learning opportunities for young people ages 10 to 15, using the following scale: 1 = poor, 2 = fair, 3 = good, 4 = excellent. Then identify areas of strength and improvement, and strategies for change.

1 2 3 4   Young adolescents are provided with a variety of one-time and/or repeat opportunities to try out different activities and involvement within your organization and within the nearby community.

1 2 3 4   Young adolescents are given the opportunity to meet and work alongside adult members of your organization through their service involvement.

1 2 3 4   Young adolescents are involved in selecting the service-learning issues and activities in which they will be involved.

1 2 3 4   Service-learning opportunities are well structured, highly involving, and designed as small- and large-group activities.

1 2 3 4   Service-learning opportunities are relationship based, providing opportunities for young adolescents to get to know one another and meet people whose experiences are different from their own.

1 2 3 4   Service-learning opportunities allow young adolescents to see quick, tangible results.

1 2 3 4   Your organization recognizes and affirms young people for their involvement in service-learning.

Strengths _____

_____

_____

_____

_____

Areas for Improvement _____

_____

_____

_____

_____

Strategies for Change _____

_____

_____

_____

_____

ARE YOUR SERVICE-LEARNING EFFORTS
APPROPRIATE FOR OLDER ADOLESCENTS?

Rate your service-learning opportunities for young people ages 16 to 18, using the following scale: 1 = poor, 2 = fair, 3 = good, 4 = excellent. Then identify areas of strength and improvement, and strategies for change.

1 2 3 4   Older adolescents are given opportunities to engage in a variety of short- and long-term service-learning programs and activities in the neighborhood, wider community, and global spheres.

1 2 3 4   Older adolescents are given the opportunity to work alongside and/or as apprentices to adults chosen for their abilities to work effectively on volunteer commitments.

1 2 3 4   Older adolescents are involved in selecting the service-learning issues and activities in which they will be involved.

1 2 3 4   The learning and reflection elements of the service-learning process help young people understand the justice issues that underlie the needs they encounter.

1 2 3 4   The service-learning sites allow older adolescents to use their unique talents or gifts under adequate adult or peer supervision.

1 2 3 4   Service-learning opportunities are geared to individuals and small groups.

1 2 3 4   Service-learning opportunities encourage older youth to meet and get to know people who are different from them.

1 2 3 4   Service-learning provides older adolescents opportunities to understand the impact that systems and institutions have on people's lives.

1 2 3 4   Service-learning helps older adolescents address social issues for the common good and understand how change takes place.

1 2 3 4   Your organization recognizes and affirms the young people for their involvement in service learning.

Strengths _____

_____

_____

_____

Areas for Improvement _____

_____

_____

_____

Strategies for Change _____

_____

_____

_____

ASSESSING SERVICE-LEARNING
THROUGH AN ASSET-BUILDING LENS

Think about your recent service experience in light of the eight categories of developmental assets identified by Search Institute. (If you can't answer some of the questions positively, write what was missing for you that made you not experience the area.)

Support—In what ways did you feel supported and cared for by:

▶ Your family? _____

_____

▶ Adult leaders? _____

_____

▶ Other youth? _____

_____

Empowerment—How did your service experience help you feel like you were making a difference for others?

_____

_____

Boundaries and Expectations—Who were positive role models for you during this experience?

_____

_____

Constructive Use of Time—How did the experience make you want to be more involved in music, arts, sports, youth activities, or religious activities? _____

_____

Commitment to Learning—How did this experience make you want to learn more or continue your education?

_____

_____

Positive Values—What kinds of positive values were reinforced for you during this experience?

_____

_____

Social Competencies—What did you learn through this experience about getting along with others?

_____

_____

Positive Identity—How did this experience make you feel good about yourself and your future?

_____

_____

CHAPTER 8

RECOGNITION: REINFORCING
THE COMMITMENT

Virtue may be its own reward, but it's also nice to get a pat on the back once in a while and thanks for a job well done. Young people especially need to be encouraged and recognized for their contributions. They also need to develop the habit of stepping back and celebrating their own accomplishments. Finally, recognition is a chance for them to think about how they can serve others in the future.

Recognition, the fourth phase in service-learning, isn't just about celebrating the good work that has been done. In fact, it should be more focused on exploring ideas and opportunities for future service. There are three key tasks of recognition:

1. Affirming and celebrating what was done;

2. Sharing learnings and commitments as a catalyst for community growth; and

3. Helping young people choose how to stay involved in the issues and stick with their commitment.

Affirming and Celebrating What Was Done

Celebration is an important component of the service-learning partnership sponsored by the Volunteer Center of Santa Cruz County in Santa Cruz, California. At the beginning of the semester, the agency throws a party for students, staff, volunteers, and parents so that they can get to know each other. Then at the end of the semester, they have another party to celebrate their accomplishments. In addi-

tion, the organization arranges for the County Board of Supervisors to host a news conference on National Youth Service Day. Students tell their stories, and public officials recognize and thank the young people for their contribution to the community.[1]

When organizations celebrate young people's accomplishments and growth, they are celebrating their own hope for the future. The passion, energy, hopefulness, and concern young people bring to and gain from service-learning are reminders of the importance of working for service and justice.

Affirmation and celebration spotlight the positive things accomplished through service-learning and how participants have personally grown as a result of the experience. It happens formally and informally to different degrees within work group, families, the organization, the agency served, and the local community. It can be planned or spontaneous—the dinner table or at an event for a group whose service has taken them out of town. Affirmation and celebration help bring participants closer to the experience and—once again—open the door to future commitments.

In addition to acknowledging young people, it is critical to honor the contributions of the many other people involved. These can include:

■ Youth and adult program leaders;

■ Families;

■ Adult allies;

- Community members;
- Agency partners;
- Organizational leaders;
- Financial supporters ; and
- Many others who help make the work successful.

In many of these cases, there are opportunities to highlight the roles that individuals play, not just in the logistics of the work, but as asset builders for the young people who were involved. Having young people tell stories about how individuals (not just the leaders) showed care, set boundaries, shared openly, and served as positive role models can reinforce the opportunity that everyone has to engage in the lives of young people.

There are dozens of ways to celebrate and affirm people's involvement in service-learning. Here are a few possibilities:

- Give young people certificates of recognition.
- Write letters to the editor thanking the young people and their supporters.
- Encourage media coverage.
- Invite community members to send letters of thanks to the young people.
- Highlight the young people's contribution during assemblies and gatherings of the organization or community.
- Have celebratory picnics, potlucks, or other parties.

Sharing Learnings and Commitments as a Catalyst for Community Growth

Part of the power of service-learning can be the impact it has on those who see the difference that young people's contributions can make. Through sharing their learning and commitments with families, organizations, and their communities, young people call others to join them in their work on behalf of service and justice.

There are many occasions and methods you can use to help young people spread the word about what they've done and what more there is to do.

Many of these methods can become the next round of service-learning action as they seek to create positive change by educating and influencing others to take action.

Presentations—Have young people come up with a list of things they would like others to know about their service-learning experience. Encourage them to include some stories to liven up their presentation. Help them draft what they want to say and divide the time so that no one dominates.

Presentations can be made to a variety of audiences. Some possible audiences include:

- Organizational leaders, councils, committees, or boards;
- Community and organization members who supported the group with encouragement and/or money;
- Families and friends;
- Other young people who didn't participate;
- Younger children;
- Groups of youth from other organizations;
- Political and community leaders;
- Activist groups; and
- Neighbors or organization members gathered in small groups.

Young people can also do presentations for individuals, families, or small groups on a more personal level.

Multimedia presentations—Young people can liven up their message by changing the medium. Possibilities include slide, video, audio, Web-based, or computer-generated presentations. You may also have access to facilities to create a program for local access cable television. These presentations can include speaking, reflective music, journal readings, stories, poems, and on-site video footage, photos, and slides.

Print presentations—Young people can write about their experiences for submission to a local newspaper. Include photos and personal reflections. Describe any follow-up activities you are planning and invite interested youth to call for details. Similar articles could be included in your organization's newsletter. Depending on the scope of the project, you could produce a report or manual on the experience and its learnings.

Mixed presentations—Many organizations have a periodic family night or seasonal meeting for parents and families to catch up on what's happening. These meetings may be appropriate settings for minipresentations on service-learning, added to the mix of stories about the latest bike trip, overnight retreat, minicourse, or other youth experiences.

Posted presentations—Create a large "poster" or bulletin board to describe your experience with photos, written reflections, stories, and other artifacts. Or mail your reports or articles to interested people.

Public reflections—Arrange for young people to offer their reflections on the service-learning experience as part of a regularly scheduled event or meeting. Or arrange for a special event to highlight the service-learning program and give young people the opportunity to tell their stories and assume roles as emcees, producers, directors, or speakers.

Reflective readings—Create a booklet of reflective readings that includes journal excerpts and other writings about the experiences. The booklet can serve as a reminder of the experience for youth participants and help family and community members learn more about what their young people were involved in.

Service resource series—Use information from this service-learning experience to create the first in a series of resource sheets on service needs and opportunities. Give people enough of the facts about the site to let them know whether it would be a good fit for them. Add enough human interest information to persuade prospective volunteers that the benefits of working with the agency clients more than compensates for any possible problems encountered on-site. Assemble the resource sheets into a binder (or Web site) that's available to interested people.

Don't wait until after the action phase is finished to plan your sharing opportunities. Scheduling them as soon after the expected conclusion of the project as possible will give young people something to look forward to (whether they are nervous or excited), and assure that their storytelling remains fresh and enthusiastic. It is also a wonderful way for youth to mark the completion of a job well done.

Personally Integrating Learnings and Commitments

During reflection young people explored how they learned, grew, and maybe even changed through service, as well as options that are available for their continued involvement with issues and concerns raised during action. They also linked their involvement with values and lifestyles. Recognition should go a step further to help them identify what it realistically will mean to integrate these values into their lives. In this sense, recognition serves as a transition for reentry into the service-learning process from a new, more committed perspective.

Taking the next concrete steps is a critical element in maintaining a commitment to a particular issue. The following list offers nine ideas for brainstorming with young people ways to deal with an issue that they were exposed to through their service-learning experience.

■ **Expanding awareness**—Young people can learn more about an issue on their own or through special projects. For example, if the issue of food stamps and other aid to families is raised during work at a shelter, young people can decide to learn more about programs in your state, who is eligible, and the positions of various politicians on the issue.

■ **Joining a justice support group**—There may be local or national groups organized to address issues raised during your project. For example, young people could decide to support a global hunger relief organization, such as Save the Children, by donating 5 percent of all money they raise through their regular fund-raisers. Or they could hold a special fund-raiser each year just for this purpose.

■ **Being an advocate**—Young people can be powerful spokespeople for those whose rights are denied or whose needs are not given adequate attention. There are two kinds of advocacy they could take on. Political advocacy focuses on letter writing and other attempts to influence policy and policy makers. Economic advocacy, such as boycotting products developed in unhealthy or oppressive environments, is another option and should be combined with awareness-raising efforts about the issue.

■ **Making lifestyle changes**—Young people can choose to share generously their time, creativity, skills, money, energy, and other resources with others. Examples include regular visits to a nursing home or hospital, donating usable items and clothing, and making a commitment to contribute financially to address an issue.

■ **Doing direct service**—Some young people decide that they want to commit to one-time, seasonal, or ongoing involvement with a project above and beyond the action phase of their service-learning program.

■ **Choosing immersion experiences**—Immersion experiences, such as work camps, give young people an opportunity to put concentrated time into service and learning about issues and needs. These experiences are several days to several weeks long and often involve travel. Examples of immersion experiences include house-building projects and volunteering at a summer camp for younger youth.

■ **Exploring career directions**—Young people can use their service experience to assess potential education and job choices. For example, after volunteering at a local hospital, one young man added Spanish to his course list so that he would be better able to communicate with the large number of Spanish-speaking patients.

■ **Forming mentoring relationships**—Mentoring relationships can take many shapes such as matching young people who are experienced with service-learning with those for whom it is a new experience, or pairing young people with professionals in careers they would like to learn more about.

■ **Incorporating service and justice commitments into personal spirituality**—In one community, young people who were involved in the cleanup of a local river were so moved by the importance of their work that they held a community ceremony that included music and readings about responsibility for the earth. Whether through prayer, meditation, or study, there are many ways to incorporate service and justice commitments into spirituality.

If a goal is to nurture in young people an ongoing commitment to service, justice, and community building, a string of individual projects may not be enough to deepen and solidify the commitment so that it becomes a lifestyle "habit" for young people. There are other important things to consider as well. Alan R. Andreason, an expert in how to encourage and support individual behavior change, suggests that there are seven elements to helping individuals maintain a positive change in their lives.[2] (We have adapted his approach to apply to service-learning.)

1. Monitor satisfaction—It is important to stay in touch with young people to see how it's going so that you can respond to disappointments or places where young people get stuck.

2. Keep expectations realistic—Don't set expectations so high (or let young people set their own expectations so high) that they get discouraged or disappointed.

3. Highlight hidden benefits—Depending on the type of action young people take, the impact can be hard to see or it can take years to reach a particular goal. So it is important to help young people see incremental changes, individual success stories, and other hidden benefits (such as new relationships and skills).

4. Improve the system—Sometimes young people can get discouraged by bureaucracies or politics or other dynamics. These are instances when you can either work to change the system or help the young person find legitimate ways to work through or around the system. There may also be times when adults need to intervene on behalf of young people.

5. Enlist the support of influencers—Young people's commitments may dwindle if they experience negative reactions from people around them. Thus, the more that can be done to create a widespread commitment to and support for service, the less likely young people will face resistance—and the more likely they will feel encouraged to keep going.

6. Emphasize ongoing skills building—As young people take on new projects with greater demands, they may need to develop new skills to prepare them for the action. Thus, it's important to return to the preparation phase of service-learning to reexamine what training and skills building are needed to prepare for the new challenge.

7. Add extrinsic incentives and rewards—For lasting change to occur, the primary motivation needs to be integral to the service that's being performed. There is a danger in adding incentives for young people's service, since it risks getting young people to commit in order to get the reward or recognition, not out of a commitment to serving others. However, rewards, recognition, and reinforcement all have a place, since

they can help to overcome inertia, help people get started, and also help maintain momentum, particularly for large, long-term goals. We highlighted some possibilities for recognition earlier in the chapter.

Renewing the Service-Learning Cycle

While recognition is the last phase in the PARR service-learning process, it's really setting the stage for beginning the process again. The celebration and recognition renew energy and commitment for taking on a new challenge. Sharing learnings with others can in itself become a service-learning project. It can also encourage new people to become engaged in service. And central to supporting young people's ongoing commitments is continuing to offer well-designed opportunities for serving others.

In short, service-learning is never really just a one-time project or program—though a particular program or project may, indeed, have a beginning and end. Rather, even if it is not formalized, service-learning at its best is an ongoing process of growth, learning, and contribution to others—a spiral that leads to deeper commitment and greater impact as young people develop the skills, and passions that will help them change the world.

POSTSCRIPT

NURTURING A GENEROUS GENERATION

Recent years have seen widespread concern about our society's overemphasis on individualism and consumerism, and our dwindling sense of shared responsibility for the well-being of others. In 1998, the National Commission on Civic Renewal graphically summarized the concern:

Too many of us have become passive and disengaged. Too many of us lack confidence in our capacity to make basic moral and civic judgments, to join with our neighbors to do the work of community, to make a difference. Never have we had so many opportunities for participation, yet rarely have we felt so powerless. . . . In a time that cries out for civic action, we are in danger of becoming a nation of spectators.[1]

It would be naive and simplistic to assert that service-learning is the answer to this situation. Hundreds of factors have led to the current concerns, and many strategies are needed to renew national commitment to the common good. Yet both service-learning and asset building clearly have much to contribute. For example, asset building can contribute to civic renewal through its focus on relationships, on rebuilding the positive, and through individual capacity and responsibility for all young people.

Service-learning offers a specific strategy for helping young people develop the commitments, skills, and attitudes that, over time, can help to reverse the sense of powerlessness and disengagement. Indeed, findings synthesized by Search Institute researchers suggest that people who volunteered as children or youth are more likely as adults to:

- Volunteer;
- Be involved in their community;
- Participate in political activities;
- Have leadership positions in community organizations; and
- Believe they can make a difference.[2]

Thus, young people who engage in service-learning are likely to become adults who are confident in their ability to make a difference—and committed to doing so. They become active contributors to their organizations, neighborhoods, community, nation, and world. They become the leaders who call everyone to a new level of commitment and compassion.

In his book *All Kids Are Our Kids,* Search Institute president Peter L. Benson writes, "Perhaps the most urgent task facing American society is rebuilding a sense of community, of village, in which everyone reclaims or accepts their shared responsibility to—and stake in—nurturing the youngest generation."[3]

As young people engage in service-learning, they are themselves engaged in opportunities that will nurture and guide them to be caring, responsible, and contributing members of society. They are also preparing themselves to be the asset builders of the future, as they pass on their commitments to serving others and building community to their children and their children's children.

125

NOTES

INTRODUCTION—EXPLORING CONNECTIONS

[1] Virginia A. Hodgkinson and Murray S. Weitzman, *Volunteering and Giving among Teenagers 12 to 17 Years of Age: Findings from a National Survey, 1996 Edition* (Washington, DC: Independent Sector, 1997), 1–2.

[2] Lloyd D. Johnston, Jerald G. Bachman, and Patrick M. O'Malley, *Monitoring the Future: Questionnaire Responses from the Nation's High School Seniors, 1995* (Ann Arbor: Institute for Social Research, University of Michigan, 1997), 86.

[3] Peter L. Benson, Peter C. Scales, Nancy Leffert, and Eugene C. Roehlkepartain, *A Fragile Foundation: The State of Developmental Assets among American Youth* (Minneapolis: Search Institute, 1999), 19.

[4] Ibid.

[5] Ibid., 140.

[6] Peter L. Benson, *All Kids Are Our Kids: What Communities Must Do to Raise Caring and Responsible Children and Adolescents* (San Francisco: Jossey-Bass, 1997), 149.

CHAPTER 1—BUILDING ASSETS FOR SERVICE LEARNING

[1] Alliance for Service-Learning in Education Reform, *Standards of Quality for School-Based and Community-Based Service-Learning* (Washington, DC: Author, 1995), 2.

[2] Robert Shumer. "Executive Summary: Describing Service-Learning: A Delphi Study" (St. Paul: University of Minnesota, 1993).

[3] Lynn Ingrid Nelson, *Helping Youth Thrive: How Youth Organizations Can—and Do—Build Developmental Assets* (Minneapolis: Search Institute, 1998), 12.

[4] Peter C. Scales, "Does Service-Learning Make a Difference?" *Source Newsletter* (January 1999), 2–3.

[5] Peter C. Scales and Nancy Leffert, *Developmental Assets: A Synthesis of the Scientific Research on Adolescent Development* (Minneapolis: Search Institute, 1999).

[6] Peter L. Benson, Peter C. Scales, Nancy Leffert, and Eugene C. Roehlkepartain, *A Fragile Foundation: The State of Developmental Assets among American Youth* (Minneapolis: Search Institute, 1999), 34.

[7] For an examination of cultural factors that have weakened the asset foundation for young people, see Peter L. Benson, *All Kids Are Our Kids: What Communities Must Do to Raise Caring and Responsible Children and Adolescents* (San Francisco, CA: Jossey-Bass, 1997).

[8] For a more comprehensive review of the research on service-learning, see Alan S. Waterman (editor), *Service-Learning: Applications from the Research* (Mahwah, NJ: Lawrence Erlbaum, 1997). Also see Robin Vue-Benson, Robert Shumer, and Madeleine S. Hengel, *Impacts and Effects of Service: Topic Bibliography* (St. Paul: National Service-Learning Cooperative Clearinghouse, University of Minnesota, 1997).

[9] Excerpt from a presentation at the 1998 Healthy Communities • Healthy Youth conference. Quoted in "Youth Speak Out!" *Assets: The Magazine of Ideas for Healthy Communities & Healthy Youth* (Winter 1998–99), 11.

[10] John P. Kretzmann and Paul H. Schmitz, "It Takes a Child to Raise a Whole Village," *Wingspread* (17, 4, Fall 1995), 8-10.

[11] Benson, *All Kids Are Our Kids,* Chapter 5.

[12] Virginia A. Hodgkinson and Murray S. Weitzman, *Volunteering and Giving among Teenagers 12 to 17 Years of Age: Findings from a National Survey, 1996 Edition* (Washington, DC: Independent Sector, 1997), 29.

[13] Ibid., 16.

[14] Shepherd Zeldin and Suzanne Tarlov, "Service-Learning as a Vehicle for Youth Development," in Joan Shine (editor), *Service Learning* (Chicago: University of Chicago Press, 1997), 183.

[15] Robert Wuthnow, *Learning to Care: Elementary Kindness in an Age of Indifference* (New York: Oxford University Press, 1995), 38.

CHAPTER 2—CULTIVATING LEADERSHIP AND SUPPORT

[1] Alliance for Service-Learning in Education Reform, *Standards of Quality for School-Based Service-Learning* (Washington, DC: Author, 1993), 10.

[2] Quoted in Rich Willits Cairn and James C. Kielsmeier (editors), *Growing Hope: A Sourcebook on Integrating Youth Service into the School Curriculum,* 1st ed. (St. Paul, MN: National Youth Leadership Council, 1991), 82.

[3] Eugene C. Roehlkepartain, *A Practical Guide for Developing Agency/School Partnerships for Service-Learning* (Washington, DC: Points of Light Foundation, 1994), 22.

4 For more on youth leadership from an asset-building perspective, see *An Asset Builder's Guide to Youth Leadership* (Minneapolis: Search Institute, 1999).

5 Excerpt from a presentation at the 1998 Healthy Communities • Healthy Youth conference. Quoted in "Youth Speak Out!" *Assets: The Magazine of Ideas for Healthy Communities & Healthy Youth* (Winter 1998–99), 11.

6 Barry Checkoway, *Young People Creating Community Change* (Battle Creek, MI: W. K. Kellogg Foundation, n.d.), 10.

7 Novella Zett Keith, "Doing Service Projects in Urban Settings," in Alan S. Waterman (editor), *Service-Learning: Applications from the Research* (Mahwah, NJ: Lawrence Erlbaum Associates, 1997), 127–149.

8 Jane Kendall, John Duley, Tom Little, Jane Permaul, and Sharon Rubin, "Strategies for Institutional and Organizational Change," in Jane C. Kendall (editor), *Combining Service and Learning: A Resource Book for Community and Public Service,* vol. 1 (Raleigh, NC: National Society for Experiential Education, 1990), 557–569.

9 Kate McPherson, "Educational Leadership for Service-Learning," in Rich Willits Cairn and James C. Kielsmeier (editors), *Growing Hope: A Sourcebook on Integrating Youth Service into the School Curriculum,* 1st ed. (St. Paul, MN: National Youth Leadership Council, 1991), 87.

CHAPTER 3—MAKING SERVICE-LEARNING WORK FOR ALL KIDS

1 "A Video Worth Its Weight in Gold," *Assets: The Magazine of Ideas for Healthy Communities & Healthy Youth* (Spring 1998), 3.

2 "Teens Keep Activities 'Off Center'—and Right on Track," *Assets* (Spring 1998), 3.

3 "Mentors Focus on Young Offenders," *Assets* (Autumn 1996), 5.

4 "On the Money: Teens Gain by Giving Grants," *Assets* (Summer 1998), 3.

5 Susan J. Ellis, Anne Weisbord, and Katherine H. Noyes, *Children as Volunteers: Preparing for Community Service,* rev. ed. (Philadelphia: Energize, 1991), 59–60.

6 Ann Shoemaker, *Teaching Young Children through Service* (St. Paul, MN: National Youth Leadership Council, 1999), 20.

7 Peter L. Benson, Peter C. Scales, Nancy Leffert, and Eugene C. Roehlkepartain, *A Fragile Foundation: The State of Developmental Assets among American Youth* (Minneapolis: Search Institute, 1999), 18–19.

8 Maryland Student Service Alliance, *Special Education Service-Learning Guide,* rev. ed. (Baltimore: Maryland Department of Education, 1993), 16.

9 Ibid., 17–24.

10 According to data from the 1992 follow-up survey of the National Education Longitudinal Study of 1988, here are the percentages of high school seniors who reported performing any community service, by income level:

First quartile (lowest income)	30 percent
Second quartile	37 percent
Third quartile	45 percent
Fourth quartile	60 percent

"Community Service Performed by High School Seniors," *National Center for Education Statistics: Educational Policy Issues: Statistical Perspectives* (October 1995).

11 David Heffernan, *Service Opportunities for Youth* (Washington, DC: Adolescent Pregnancy Clearinghouse, Children's Defense Fund, 1989), 5.

12 Anne Lewis, "Urban Youth in Community Service: Becoming Part of the Solution," *ERIC Clearinghouse on Urban Education Digest* (September 1992), 1.

13 Dale A. Blyth, Rebecca Saito, and Tom Berkas, "A Quantitative Study of the Impact of Service-Learning Programs," in Alan S. Waterman (editor), *Service-Learning: Applications from the Research* (Mahwah, NJ: Lawrence Erlbaum Associates, 1997), 53.

14 Novella Zett Keith, "Doing Service Projects in Urban Settings," in Alan S. Waterman (editor), *Service-Learning: Applications from the Research* (Mahwah, NJ: Lawrence Erlbaum Associates, 1997), 142.

15 For more information on service-learning with vulnerable youth, see Robin Vue-Benson and Rob Shumer, *Topic Bibliography: Service-Learning Connections to Resiliency and "At-Risk" Youth* (St. Paul, MN: National Information Clearinghouse for Service-Learning, 1994).

16 A Search Institute study of mainline Protestant congregations found that family service projects are one of the three types of family experiences that contribute to growth in faith. See Eugene C. Roehlkepartain, *The Teaching Church: Moving Christian Education to Center Stage* (Nashville, TN: Abingdon Press, 1993), 170.

17 "Family Volunteering Creates Meaningful Holidays," press release from the Family Matters program of the Points of Light Foundation (November 9, 1995).

18 *Family Matters: The First Year* (Washington, DC: Points of Light Foundation, 1992).

19 Lorine Matters, *Intergenerational Relations: Older Adults and Youth. County Extension Program Guide* (Columbia: Center on Rural Elderly, University of Missouri, 1990), 6–7.

CHAPTER 4—SETTING THE STAGE FOR SERVICE-LEARNING

1 Barry Fenstermacher, "Infusing Service-Learning into the Curriculum," in Jane C. Kendall and associates, *Combining Service and Learning: A Resource Book for Community and Public Service,* vol. 2 (Raleigh, NC: National Society for Experiential Education, 1990), 195.

2 Janet Eyler and Dwight Giles Jr., "The Importance of Program Quality in Service-Learning," in Alan S. Waterman (editor), *Service-Learning: Applications from the Research* (Mahwah, NJ: Lawrence Erlbaum Associates, 1997), 67.

3 Alliance for Service-Learning in Education Reform, *Standards of Quality for School-Based Service-Learning* (Washington, DC: Author, 1993), 6.

4 John Dewey, *School and Society,* 2nd ed.(Chicago: University of Chicago Press, 1933).

5 Eugene C. Roehlkepartain, *A Practical Guide for Developing Agency/School Partnerships for Service-Learning* (Washington, DC: Points of Light Foundation, 1995), 23.

6 Cited in "Knock, Knock: Should Kids Sell Candy to Strangers?" *Youth Today* (October 1998), 39.

[7] Linda M. Frank, *Student Service and Philanthropy Project: A Resource Guide for Establishing a Student-Run Foundation* (New York: Surdna Foundation, 1994).

[8] Nonprofit Risk Management Center, 1001 Connecticut Ave., NW, Suite 900, Washington, DC 20036-5504; 202-785-3891; www.nonprofitrisk.org.

[9] National Collaboration for Youth, *Screening Volunteers to Prevent Child Sexual Abuse: A Community Guide for Youth Organizations* (Washington, DC: National Assembly of National Voluntary Health and Social Welfare Organizations, 1997).

[10] Ibid., 19.

[11] Ibid., 19.

[12] Ibid., 14.

CHAPTER 5—PREPARATION: GETTING READY TO SERVE

[1] The Wirthlin Group, *The Prudential Spirit of Community Youth Survey* (Newark, NJ: Prudential Insurance Company of America, 1995), 9.

[2] Dale A. Blyth, Rebecca Saito, and Tom Berkas, "A Quantitative Study of the Impact of Service-Learning Programs," in Alan S. Waterman (editor), *Service-Learning: Applications from the Research* (Mahwah, NJ: Lawrence Erlbaum, 1997), 52.

[3] Virginia A. Hodgkinson and Murray S. Weitzman, *Volunteering and Giving among Teenagers 12 to 17 Years of Age, 1996 Edition* (Washington, DC: Independent Sector, 1997), 4.

[4] "The Power of Youth," *Ziv Tzedakah Fund Report* (April 1, 1999), 5–6. Also see the school's Web site: www.digitalrag.com/iqbal/.

[5] From the organization's Web site: www.giraffe.org

[6] "Teens Triumph over Techno-Tribulations," *Assets: The Magazine of Ideas for Healthy Communities & Healthy Youth* (Autumn 1998), 3.

[7] Peter C. Scales, "Does Service-Learning Make a Difference?" *Source Newsletter* (January 1999), 2.

[8] James Toole and Pamela Toole, "Reflection as a Tool for Turning Service Experience into Learning Experiences," in Carol W. Kinsley and Kate McPherson (editors), *Enriching the Curriculum through Service-Learning* (Alexandria, VA: Association for Supervision and Curriculum Development, 1995), 105.

[9] Eugene C. Roehlkepartain, *A Practical Guide for Developing Agency/School Partnerships for Service-Learning* (Washington, DC: Points of Light Foundation, 1995), 89.

[10] Barry Checkoway, *Adults as Allies* (Battle Creek, MI: W. K. Kellogg Foundation, n.d.), 25.

CHAPTER 6—ACTION: MAKING A DIFFERENCE

[1] Dan Conrad and Diane Hedin, *Youth Service: A Guidebook for Developing and Operating Effective Programs* (Washington, DC: Independent Sector, 1987), 39.

CHAPTER 7—REFLECTION: MINING MEANING FROM EXPERIENCE

[1] James Toole and Pamela Toole, "Reflection as a Tool for Turning Service Experience into Learning Experiences," in Carol W. Kinsley and Kate McPherson (editors), *Enriching the Curriculum through Service-Learning* (Alexandria, VA: Association for Supervision and Curriculum Development, 1995), 99–100.

[2] Dale A. Blyth, Rebecca Saito, and Tom Berkas, "A Quantitative Study of the Impact of Service-Learning Programs," in Alan S. Waterman (editor), *Service-Learning: Applications from the Research* (Mahwah, NJ: Lawrence Erlbaum, 1997), 51–52.

[3] Janet Eyler and Dwight Giles Jr., "The Importance of Program Quality in Service-Learning," in Waterman, 57–76.

[4] Toole and Toole, "Reflection as a Tool" 108.

[5] Ibid., 107–108.

[6] Maryland Student Service Alliance, *Special Education Service-Learning Guide,* rev. ed. (Baltimore: Maryland Department of Education, 1993), 250.

[7] Harry Silcox, *A How-to Guide to Reflection: Adding Cognitive Learning to Community Service Programs* (Philadelphia: Brighton Press, 1993), 81.

[8] Kate McPherson, *Learning through Service* (Mt. Vernon, WA: Project Service Leadership, 1989).

[9] Dan Conrad and Diane Hedin, *Youth Service: A Guidebook for Developing and Operating Effective Programs* (Washington, DC: Independent Sector, 1986), 46–49.

CHAPTER 8—RECOGNITION: REINFORCING THE COMMITMENT

[1] Eugene C. Roehlkepartain, *A Practical Guide for Developing Agency/School Partnerships for Service-Learning* (Washington, DC: Points of Light Foundation 1995), 125–26.

[2] Alan R. Andreasen, *Marketing Social Change* (San Francisco: Jossey-Bass, 1995).

POSTSCRIPT—NURTURING A GENEROUS GENERATION

[1] National Commission on Civic Renewal, *A Nation of Spectators: How Civic Disengagement Weakens America and What We Can Do about It* (College Park: Institute for Philosophy and Public Policy, University of Maryland of College Park, 1998), www.puafedu/civicrenewal.

[2] Peter C. Scales and Nancy Leffert, *Developmental Assets: A Synthesis of the Scientific Research on Adolescent Development* (Minneapolis: Search Institute, 1999), Chapter 2.

[3] Peter L. Benson, *All Kids Are Our Kids: What Communities Must Do to Raise Caring and Responsible Children and Adolescents* (San Francisco: Jossey-Bass, 1997), 103.

ADDITIONAL SERVICE-LEARNING RESOURCES

There are dozens of national and regional organizations dedicated to service-learning and related topics, and there are literally hundreds of publications and Web sites with helpful information. The following resources are just a sampling of the helpful material that is available for schools, congregations, youth organizations, and others who seek to engage children and youth in service-learning.

NATIONAL ORGANIZATIONS

Corporation for National Service, 1201 New York Avenue, Northwest, Washington, DC 20525; (202) 606-5000; www.cns.gov. The corporation sponsors Learn and Serve America, which supports service-learning projects in schools. Its Web site includes extensive news about the history of and federal support for youth service, and the Learn and Serve America section lists service-learning contacts in all 50 states.

Do Something, 423 West 55th Street, 8th Floor, New York, NY 10019; (212) 523-1175; www.dosomething.org. Founded on the belief that positive change is possible and that young people have the power to create that change, Do Something offers a variety of national programs to inspire young people to action, including the annual BRICK Award for Community Leadership, which honors young leaders who are rebuilding community.

National Youth Leadership Council, 1910 West County Road B, St. Paul, MN 55113; (651) 631-3672; www.nylc.org. NYLC is a leading advocate and resource center for service-learning, particularly in schools. The organization sponsors an annual service-learning conference and publishes *Generator,* a journal on service-learning.

Points of Light Foundation, 1737 H Street, Northwest, Washington, DC 20006 (202) 223-9168; www.pointsoflight.org. The foundation's youth and education outreach area provides programs, products, and services related to youth service, service-learning, and youth leadership. It has a particular focus on the role of community agencies in service-learning. Points of Light also sponsors the Family Matters program, which focuses on family volunteering.

Youth Service America, 1101 15th Street, Northwest, Suite 200, Washington, DC 20005; (202) 296-2992; www.servenet.org/ysa. Youth Service America is a resource center and alliance of more than 200 organizations "committed to increasing the quantity and quality of opportunities for young Americans to serve locally, nationally, or globally." Among other programs and activities, it sponsors National Youth Service Day every April, which engages more than two million young people in service each year.

PUBLICATIONS

Beyond Leaf Raking: Learning to Serve/Serving to Learn, by Peter L. Benson and Eugene C. Roehlkepartain (Nashville: Abingdon Press, 1993). This comprehensive guide to service-learning in Christian congregations emphasizes the importance of planning and reflection in ensuring that youth service contributes to young people's personal and spiritual development.

Combining Service and Learning: A Resource Book for Community and Public Service, by Jane C. Kendall and Associates (Raleigh, NC: National Society for Experiential Education, 1990). This three-volume collection of essays and case studies examines many dimensions of service-learning history, theory, and practice.

Creating and Managing Partnerships for Service-Learning: A Guide for Service-Learning Coordinators, by Jim Pitofsky (Alexandria, VA: National Association for Partners in Education, 1994). This manual examines the many facets of forming a school-community partnership for service-learning.

Doing Self-Directed Study for Service-Learning, by Robert Shumer and Thomas H. Berkas (St. Paul, MN: National Service-Learning Clearinghouse, 1992). This monograph guides service-learning practitioners in doing self-evaluation of their programs. It provides worksheets and exercises that help to shape an evaluation.

Enriching the Curriculum through Service Learning, edited by Carol W. Kinsley and Kate McPherson (Alexandria, VA: Association for Supervision and Curriculum Development, 1995). This book gathers short essays and practical ideas on the specific dynamics of integrating service-learning into a school's curriculum.

Growing Hope: A Sourcebook on Integrating Youth Service into the School Curriculum, edited by Rich Willits Cairn and James C. Kieslmeier (St. Paul, MN: National Youth Leadership Council, 1991). This comprehensive collection of articles, essays, and tips offers extensive practical advice as well as concrete case studies on service-learning in schools.

A Kid's Guide to Social Action, by Barbara A. Lewis (Minneapolis: Free Spirit, 1991). This comprehensive, award-winning book gives young people all the tools they need to take on social issues that concern them.

Learning to Care: Elementary Kindness in an Age of Indifference, by Robert Wuthnow (New York: Oxford University Press, 1995). Though not specifically about service-learning, this resource examines the dynamics in families, institutions, and society that nurture in young people a commitment to caring for others.

A Practical Guide for Developing Agency/School Partnerships for Service-Learning, by Eugene C. Roehlkepartain (Washington, DC: Points of Light Foundation, 1993). This notebook covers the service-learning process from the perspective of community agencies that engage youth in service-learning.

Service Learning, edited by Joan Schine (Chicago: University of Chicago Press, 1997). This publication of the National Society for the Study of Education presents a variety of essays on the theory and research that undergird service-learning.

Service-Learning: Applications from the Research, edited by Alan S. Waterman (Mahwah, NJ: Lawrence Erlbaum Associates, 1997). This book summarizes current research on service-learning and the implications of that research for practitioners.

Teaching Young Children through Service, by Ann Shoemaker (St. Paul, MN: National Youth Leadership Council, 1999). In addition to summarizing strategies for doing service-learning with 4- to 8-year-olds, this book offers numerous service project ideas for young children.

Volunteering and Giving among Teenagers 12 to 17 Years of Age, 1996 Edition, by Virginia A. Hodgkinson and Murray S. Weitzman (Washington, DC: Independent Sector, 1997). This report presents the findings of Independent Sector's latest poll on youth engagement in service to others.

Youth Service: A Guidebook for Developing and Operating Effective Programs, by Dan Conrad and Diane Hedin (Washington, DC: Independent Sector, 1987). This guide is packed with the practical wisdom of two of the pioneers in service-learning.

WEB SITES

Giraffe Project (www.giraffe.org/giraffe). Designed to encourage people to "stick their necks out for the common good," this site includes stories and quotes to motivate people to help others and build community.

K-12 Education in Philanthropy Project (www.msu.edu/~k12phil/). This project focuses on developing curricula and tools that teach students about the nonprofit sector in U.S. society while building the skills young people need through service-learning. Includes great quotes and stories in the "Resource Room."

Learn, Serve, and Surf (www.edb.utexas.edu/servicelearning). Created by a graduate student at the University of Texas, this site overviews K-12 service-learning, connects to Web sites that integrate Internet use with service-learning, and has links to other service-learning sites and online discussion groups.

National Service-Learning Clearinghouse (www.nicsl.coled.umn.edu). Funded by the Corporation for National Service, this site focuses on all dimensions of service-learning, covering kindergarten through higher education. It includes a comprehensive database on service-learning.

ServeNet (www.servenet.org). Sponsored by Youth Service America, this site seeks to network among organizations that engage youth in service and to provide quality information on youth service to volunteer-based organizations.

Youth in Action (www.mightymedia.com). This site for youth focuses on human rights and the environment, offering users tools to research topics, plan action, and connect with others through chat rooms.

Youthlink (www.youthlink.org). This organization is dedicated to building alliances between youth and adults to invest in the future. It includes a valuable "Action Guide" that can be downloaded.

ADDITIONAL ASSET-BUILDING RESOURCES

Search Institute offers a variety of additional resources on developmental assets and asset building for individuals, organizations, and communities. For information on resources that are currently available, contact:

Search Institute
700 South Third Street, Suite 210
Minneapolis, MN 55415
800-888-7828
www.search-institute.org

ABOUT THE CONTRIBUTORS

Eugene C. Roehlkepartain is director of publishing and communication for Search Institute. He is author or coauthor of several books and manuals on service-learning, including *Beyond Leaf Raking: Learning to Serve / Serving to Learn* (Abingdon Press), *Everyone Wins When Youth Serve* (Points of Light Foundation), *Kids Have a Lot to Give: How Congregations Can Nurture Habits of Giving and Serving for the Common Good* (Search Institute), *and A Practical Guide for Developing Agency/School Partnerships for Service-Learning* (Points of Light Foundation). He has also written extensively on asset building.

Thomas Bright is the service justice coordinator at the Center for Ministry Development in Naugatuck, Connecticut. In addition to writing and speaking extensively about service and justice issues within the Roman Catholic tradition, Bright oversees the center's national service-learning program, Young Neighbors in Action, which each summer engages almost 2,000 young people in intensive service-learning experiences.

Beth Margolis-Rupp is the service-learning coordinator for the Radnor School District, Radnor, Pennsylvania, and director of the Service-Learning Institute at the Jewish Community High School of Gratz College. She has served as a Kellogg Peer Consultant for service-learning.

ABOUT SEARCH INSTITUTE

Search Institute is an independent, nonprofit, nonsectarian organization whose mission is to advance the well-being of children and youth by generating knowledge and promoting its application. Search Institute conducts research and evaluation, develops publications and practical tools, and provides training and technical assistance. The institute collaborates with others to promote long-term organizational and cultural change that supports the healthy development of all children and adolescents.

The institute developed the framework of developmental assets in 1990. It supports communities and organizations in their asset-building efforts through its Healthy Communities • Healthy Youth initiative. In addition, the institute has conducted several studies of the impact of service-learning in partnership with the National Youth Leadership Council, St. Paul, Minnesota.

For a free information packet on Search Institute, call 800-888-7828. Or visit our Web site: www.search-institute.org